Alpha Leadership

Tools for business leaders who want more from life

Anne Deering

Robert Dilts

Julian Russell

JOHN WILEY & SONS, LTD

Other Wiley Editorial Offices

John Wiley & Sons, Inc., 605 Third Avenue,
New York, NY 10158-0012, USA

WILEY-VCH GmbH, Pappelallee 3,
D-69469 Weinheim, Germany

John Wiley & Sons Australia Ltd, 33 Park Road, Milton,
Queensland 4064, Australia

John Wiley & Sons (Asia) Pte Ltd, 2 Clementi Loop #02-01,
Jin Xing Distripark, Singapore 129809

John Wiley & Sons (Canada) Ltd, 22 Worcester Road,
Rexdale, Ontario M9W 1L1, Canada

British Library Cataloguing in Publication Data

A catalogue record for this book is available from the British Library

ISBN 0-470-84483-3

Typeset in 11/15pt Goudy by Dorwyn Ltd, Rowlands Castle, Hants.
Printed and bound in Great Britain by Biddles Ltd, Guildford and King's Lynn.
This book is printed on acid-free paper responsibly manufactured from sustainable forestry, in which at least two trees are planted for each one used for paper production.

Why Alpha?

Alpha has a lot of different meanings, and strikes a number of different chords for us. All resonate with what we mean by Alpha Leadership.

- The beginning
  - a starting point
  - not yet there
  - the first step of a journey
- Success
  - top of the class
  - excellence
  - achievement of goals
- Alpha rhythms of the brain
  - state of relaxed alertness
  - receptivity
  - imagination flowing freely
- Alpha male
  - leader of the pack
  - strength
  - assertiveness
- Alpha female
  - leader of the community
  - role model
  - authority
- Alpha courses
  - a spiritual awakening
  - there's more to life than this
  - rejuvenation

Contents

The Alternative Contents

Preface

Julian

For a number of years I have been asking myself two questions: 'How can I help leaders appreciate the contribution their own personal development makes to increasing their value to the business?' and 'How can I help leaders understand that leadership presence, stature and influence are most easily enhanced at a psychological level?'

I have been on a long journey exploring these questions, and have created a small leadership coaching firm called PPD Consulting to help answer them. Two of my most significant influences along the way have been Robert Dilts and Anne Deering.

Since he was a student 20 or so years ago, Robert has been a pioneer of an applied psychology toolkit called neuro-linguistic programming (NLP). He has made NLP available to a broad range of professional audiences and, in particular, he has made it accessible to business consultants, trainers and coaches. Thanks to his pioneering work, NLP tools are now widely accepted as being essential to a business trainer's toolkit. In short, Robert is one of the most prolific authors and thinkers I have ever met.

Anne is a vice president at the consulting firm A. T. Kearney, the firm you call in to deliver value to your business, or if you need to restructure your organization to take advantage of a new technology or a changing market. Anne works at the hard end of business consulting, and is someone who epitomizes many of the relationship management and leadership qualities spoken about in this book. She coaches leaders who are about to go into battle, or are already in the midst of it, with extraordinary sensitivity, compassion, and courage. In addition to all of this, Anne has managed the Kearney hub for intellectual capital, bringing new consulting approaches into the firm.

All three of us share a passion about integrating the 'outer' and the 'inner' dimensions of leadership. The 'outer' dimensions concern how you shape and manage a business to achieve its objectives in the marketplace. The 'inner' dimensions concern how you organize yourself psychologically to be alert to your environment, to have a presence or stature that makes people want to follow you, the thinking skills to know what is important, and the influence to encourage people to give of their best.

The vigorous and enjoyable conversations that have led us to write this book have enhanced the way in which I work with leaders to integrate these dimensions. I hope this book increases your personal satisfaction and your value to your organization.

Robert

There is a common legend in the Silicon Valley area of San Francisco, where I was born and raised, about powerful and successful businesses and business ideas that started out as scribbles on the back of a napkin over dinner and drinks. That is indeed how this book started; except that it was a paper tablecloth instead of a napkin.

Anne, Julian and I share a common passion for leadership, and the positive influence it can have on people, companies and the world. We had all been involved in leadership, including coaching business leaders, for a number of years and had established a friendship as a result of common projects and interests. On one of my trips to London a couple of years ago, we met for dinner. As we shared ideas and experiences, the vision of a leadership book began to emerge. As we talked, we made notes and sketched out key themes and ideas on the tablecloth. Each idea that we shared seemed to spark another idea, insight or 'aha', and we quickly reached one of those peak experiences of 'flow'. By the time dinner was over, we realized we had the makings of an exciting new approach to leadership that brought together both leading edge principles and pragmatic tools that could make a profound difference in the day-to-day experience of managers struggling to keep up with a changing economy and a changing world.

Determined to follow up on this initial flash of insight and enthusiasm, we continued meeting whenever we could. These periodic meetings switched to weekly international teleconferences as we approached the final stages of writing and editing.

The result is the book you are holding now. This book arose as a result of experience, passion, mutual respect, insight, shared vision, commitment and teamwork between the authors, and these qualities are precisely what we hope the book brings into your life and into the teams and companies with which you work.

Anne

I am 42, mother of two small boys (Sam, aged four and Ben, aged three) and a 7-month-old baby, Sophie. I am also a management consultant – a demanding job, with long hours, lots of travel and high pressure to deliver against tight deadlines.

About two years ago, the tension I had felt for a long time between work and home – between doing well in my career and actually knowing what went on at nursery school; between dedicating all my non-working hours to the children and actually having some time for myself; between doing what was right from one point of view but seemed wrong from the other – became intolerable.

Then I started working with a coach, Julian Russell. Within a few months, I felt a sense of what I can only describe as peace. I felt aligned with what was important to me, there was a greater sense of congruence in how I spent my time, and I made choices with more confidence. All of this contributed to a profound transformation of my experience of work.

Applying this thinking with my clients, I found that these lessons and approaches had a significant impact on their ability to lead complex organizations, and on their sense of fulfilment.

As Julian and I reflected on our shared experience, and then talked about it and about the changing nature of work with our friend, Robert Dilts, we set out on the journey that has culminated in this book. It is our attempt to share the models and approaches we have developed in the hope that they may also help you in your search for a more integrated and successful life.

Acknowledgements

Two thinkers have provided the starting point for this book: Kevin Kelly with his seminal article and book, *New Rules for the New Economy*, and Margaret Wheatley with her ground-breaking *Leadership and the New Science*. Reading these texts made us start to consider what leaders should do differently to respond to the challenges they describe. We are indebted to both for their inspiration.

Many other thinkers and writers have contributed to our research, including Joel Barker, Richard Bandler, Gregory Bateson, Wayne Bukan, Ram Charan, Stephen Covey, Jim Collins, Ian Cunningham, Chris Edwards, John Grinder, Charles Hampden-Turner, Bill Isaacs, Jasper Kunde, Kelly Marks, Jerry Porras, Mel Scott and J.D. Thompson. For their creativity and generosity with their ideas, thank you.

For their energy and enthusiasm in reviewing and helping us to refine early versions of this book, many thanks to Hamish Bryce, John Higgins, Louis Scenti and David Thompson. Too many people helped us with the title for us to mention them all – you know who you are. Thank you!

To the people who put in so much hard work in making this book a reality, our gratitude, especially to our friends at Wiley – Claire Plimmer, Karen Weller, Rachel Wilkie, Peter Hudson, Melissa Cox, Ellie Gilbertson, Jenny Athanasiadou and Suzan Wiggins for their superb graphics and patience with endless adjustments; Claudia Goddard and Joyce Adams for their tireless support and cheerfulness; Jenny D'Angelo for her keen eye and warm encouragement; Tanyia Brown for her loving care which created the time in which to write.

Most especially our thanks go to Tom Lloyd for his professionalism, expertise and creativity.

To our friends and supporters, John Dilts, Myriam Kamhi, Ewa and Chris Robertson, thank you for keeping us sane and on the right path.

And most of all, our love and appreciation to our partners and families, Angus, Sam, Ben, Sophie, Cynthia, Anne, Martin, Anita, Andrew and Julia, for being there and helping us grow.

Introduction

This book describes a new model of leadership. We call it *Alpha Leadership*.

The approaches and tools we present here offer you ways to be successful as a business leader, ways to reduce stress and to promote happiness, at a time when these goals seem impossible for most people struggling to make sense of the workplace and its demands.

Alpha Leadership is a product of conversations between the three authors about what makes a leader successful – a sharing of case studies and research that has taken place over the last four years, during a period of unprecedented change in the business environment.

Despite our different backgrounds and experience, we were struck by the commonality in our research on successful leaders. It seemed that a new set of basic themes of leadership was emerging, that was consistent on both sides of the Atlantic, across traditional businesses as diverse as manufacturing and financial services, dot.coms through boom and bust, and the emergent dot.corps.

Our work showed that those who have led their organizations to survive and thrive in a turbulent world excelled in three separate but related dimensions that we call Anticipate, Align and Act.

By 'anticipate' we mean the ability and the eagerness to detect and respond to weak signals or trends, in order to 'get ahead of the curve'. Successful leaders have the mental agility to respond appropriately to these signals, and create organizations fluid enough to respond quickly to new circumstances.

By 'align' we mean achieving congruence in your own values and desires, and the values and desires of others, so that you can create coalitions and aligned organizations able to act effectively in pursuit of the business's goals.

Much management effort is being devoted these days to winning hearts and minds, and inducing people to commit to visions and missions, in the belief that belief itself will galvanize effective action. Usually, however, the visions stimulate nothing but apathy. As a senior executive said to us recently, 'I pull every lever available to me in the organization and nothing happens. It's like pushing on Jello, it just springs back.' The Alpha test of effective leadership is the degree to which people's *feet* are engaged and, more importantly, the direction in which they are walking.

In other words, anticipation and alignment are worth nothing without appropriate and timely action. Ultimately, actions are all that separate business winners from losers. By 'Act' we mean establishing what is important to achieve the business's goals, and doggedly persisting in areas that make a difference.

At the heart of all three dimensions lie clarity and constancy of purpose – the business's *and* the leader's. Successful leaders focus and stretch the business's goals, are clear about how the business creates value and have a strong sense of connection between their personal mission and their business role.

Alpha Leadership is our attempt to describe and synthesize these themes.

The genesis of an idea

We developed the Alpha Leadership model based on a wide range of research and experience. We have each worked with business leaders for more than 15 years, from Silicon Valley to rust belt industries, in the United

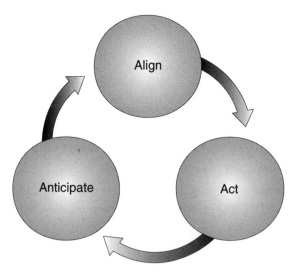

Figure Int. I   *Alpha Leadership*

States, Europe and Asia, and in contexts as diverse as traditional management consultancy, the development of a psychological discipline (Neuro-Linguistic Programming) and its application in business, dot.com venture 'catalysm' and funding, and the modelling of leadership behaviour spanning decades of business performance.

As our conclusions took shape, we became increasingly convinced that traditional approaches to leadership place far too much emphasis on action, and not nearly enough emphasis on anticipation and alignment. It is the volatility of the environments, and the networked, knowledge-based nature of the organizations in which action has to be taken, that make anticipation and alignment so crucial. We observed that leadership skills that are key to success in today's corporate world are not taught in business schools, are rarely discussed by business academics, and are not recognized within corporations as they recruit, promote and train their staff.

We noticed that business conversation was all about the 'war for talent' – and yet the solutions presented were all 'outside-in' (what the corporation needed to do to ensure people stayed, to 'make' their values align, to retain them) rather than 'inside-out' (the alignment of an individual's sense of purpose with how he or she spends time at work, and the fit of an individual's skills to the demands of the job).

In writing this book we sought to fill some of these gaps in the lexicon of leadership.

Work–life balance?

It is impossible to write a book about leadership in the 21st century without making reference to work–life balance. The statistics are daunting: 76% of managers want to spend more time with their families; 50% say they feel too mentally and physically exhausted to do anything but work or sleep; 30% say their lives are out of control; one in five say they are too stressed to enjoy their lives at all.[1]

And yet we have never been more materially successful: we earn more than ever before, we have more purchasing power, more leisure travel and our children have more material possessions.

So what is going wrong? An extreme imbalance seems to be at work, where success in the workplace spells dismal failure in other parts of our lives. We are all familiar with the symptoms of today's executive malaise –

knowing the airport lounge better than your own living room, pushing the 'door close' button on the lift because five seconds is too long a wait, children who are happier being comforted after a nightmare by granny, nanny or the babysitter (just about anyone but you, the parent), the overwhelming sense of overload and the desperate feeling that there is no way out.

There is a way out. We believe that with a new definition of leadership, and with some practical tools and approaches that can be readily applied in our daily lives as leaders, we can take control over our business lives and enjoy living them again. We need a different model of business leadership if company leaders are to learn how to do their job of making things happen, without becoming what one senior executive's spouse called 'vice president of long hours and no fun'.

It is not work that is the problem. It is the way we manage and prioritize work, and the need for alignment between what really matters to us and how we spend our waking hours.

We believe that 'work–life balance' is itself a misnomer. Work is clearly an important part of life, and it is unhelpful to polarize it as something other than, and at odds with, the rest of our lives. We believe the answer lies in integration rather than balance, making sense of our work lives so that we understand and accept how the hours invested at work fit into our overall sense of purpose, and learning how to work smart rather than hard, so that we can release time from work to be spent at home, at leisure and in the community.

The tools and approaches in the chapters that follow will help you to achieve these aims.

Tips for navigation

Alpha Leadership takes an 'inside-out' view of leadership, starting with the individual and his or her values and sense of purpose, rather than the conventional 'outside-in' approach, which holds up examples of great leaders that all aspiring leaders should try to emulate, irrespective of what kind of people they are and what kind of situations they find themselves in.

Our aim was to write a practical, 'how to' book, derived from our experience of one-to-one executive coaching, leadership development, start-up company greenhouses and business consulting. We provide readers with ideas, tools, approaches and frameworks that will help them perform better as business leaders and feel better as human beings.

Each chapter starts with a parable or story, which usually has nothing much to do with business, but which we believe sheds interesting light on issues and problems facing business leaders. This is followed by a 'sense making' section that interprets the story and relates it to real-life examples. Each chapter ends with a set of tools designed to help you develop, exploit and adapt the ideas and concepts covered by the chapter.

In accordance with the journalistic rule 'say what you're going to say, say it, and then say what you've said', the book begins with this introduction to the book's main themes, explores them in detail in three parts under the headings 'Anticipate', 'Align' and 'Act', and ends with a short, concluding chapter sketching out the overall shape and content of *Alpha Leadership*.

Part I focuses on 'anticipation'. Chapter 1, Detecting Weak Signals, examines the dilemma created by the conflict between ensuring that action is both appropriate and timely in a rapidly changing business environment. For action to be appropriate, it must be based on an intimate understanding of the circumstances, but action will only be timely if it is taken before the circumstances become clear.

Only by detecting and reacting to the 'weak signals' that precede the strong can company leaders keep the organizations in their care on the leading rather than on the trailing edge of business evolution. Weak signals must be their 'stock-in-trade' because, by the time business opportunities or threats are clear and unambiguous, it is too late to exploit or evade them.

In Chapter 2, Developing Mental Agility, we look at some of the qualities necessary for leaders to be able to respond to weak signals effectively. Mental agility is the basic requirement, but it is not enough on its own. Leaders also need open spaces to be mentally agile within. Agile leaders see the circumstances that confront them from a variety of perspectives. They are fixed in their purpose, they constantly reevaluate their goals, and are extremely flexible in the means they adopt to achieve those goals. They know when to be unusually creative within the bounds of their current objectives, and when to leap over those boundaries and propose something entirely new. They equip themselves with a range of options, and they keep as many as possible of those options open, for as long as possible.

Chapter 3, Freeing-up Resources, focuses on the qualities organizations need if the mental agility of their leaders is to make things happen.

However sensitive they are to weak signals, and however flexible they are when interpreting them, leaders will be unable to trigger timely and appropriate action unless their organizations can rechannel energy and redeploy resources, quickly. When resources are 'locked up' in existing assignments by structures, rules or habits, the organization will be unable to respond to opportunities and threats effectively, and its powers of 'self-organization' will be frustrated.

The relationship between the leader and the led is so fundamental that we devote the whole of Part II to it. The theme in these three chapters is 'alignment': the mostly tacit negotiations that go on between the leader and the led, the outcomes of which form the basis of their relationship and so determine the 'leadability' of the organization. Leaders must find ways to stimulate *concerted*, as well as appropriate and timely action. Everyone has to be ready to act effectively and quickly. The whole organization has to be on the surfboard, waiting for the wave before the crest forms.

In Chapter 4, Leading Through Embodiment, we look at the contribution the leader's personality and style can make to the alignment of an organization. The central idea in the story of Monty Roberts, the 'Horse Whisperer', is that although horses will run away from strange humans at the slightest provocation, they will follow and 'join up' with interesting humans who appear to pose no threat to them.[2] We share with horses a desire to join up, join in and be part of something. We shy away from forceful demands for loyalty and commitment, but we flock to and swarm round focal points where 'cool stuff' seems either to be happening or about to happen. Good leaders work with our hunger to involve ourselves, with others, in interesting work and exciting projects. They influence and seduce, rather than command, and try to become 'attractors', as complexity scientists put it – the embodiments of attractive energy, the centre of the swarm.

But leaders can only be attractive, in this sense, when they themselves are truly aligned. Alignment starts from the inside, out: being sure of who you are and what your 'calling' is, understanding and projecting your values and abilities, and ensuring that these inner qualities and resources are fully aligned. In short, there is no substitute for being an authentic and coherent person. That is not to say you need to be perfect: your faults don't matter if you know what you are good at, work on your weaknesses and don't pretend to be anything you are not. Just as horses will only follow if you look like you know where you're going, and it looks like a good place to go, so, too,

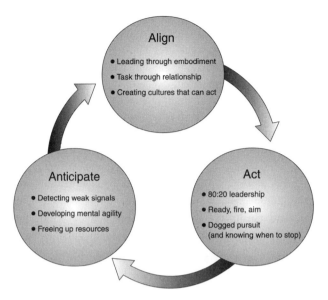

Figure Int. 2 *The nine principles of Alpha Leadership*

today's leaders need a high degree of internal alignment before they start asking others to follow them.

Chapter 5, Task Through Relationship, shifts the focus from the leader to the relationship between the leader and the led. We explore the distinction made by Mary Parker Follett between 'power over', and 'power with'. Follett was the first management writer to address the difficult problem of authority in business, and to question the 'right' a leader has to issue orders. She concluded that 'one person should not give orders to another person . . . both should agree to take their orders from the situation'.[3]

The so-called 'war for talent' is evidence that many modern company leaders are routinely flouting Follett's 'law of the situation', by failing to take fully into account the wider interests of their employees.

Chapter 6, Creating Cultures That Can Act, concludes Part II by bringing leader and led together again, and exploring the cultures that emerge from their relationships. We argue that not all organizations that are aligned with the laws of the situation and have leaders who can anticipate, acquire cultures that can *act*.

Rogues and mavericks play a vital role in action-oriented cultures, because there is a tendency for organizations to become wedded to assumptions about the way they do business and their strengths and weaknesses. These embedded (often unconscious) mental models and points of view need to be reviewed regularly if the organization is to remain healthy and alert. Rogues and mavericks can keep their organizations honest, but only when the leader values them and acknowledges their right to speak out and criticize.

Cultures that can act are 'open' in the sense that dissent is treated as a vital part of the organization's nervous system. Existing mental models and points of view are always provisional and subject to continuous revision when new information, however weak the signal, is received that casts some doubt on their validity.

Part III focuses on action. Chapter 7, 80:20 Leadership, explores the need for leaders to find time and space to think deeply about priorities. It is important to 'do things right', but it is equally important to 'do the right things', and 'in the right order'. The difficulty is that leaders must be perceived by the led to have mastered the day-to-day detail if they are also to be seen as credible priority setters. If the led believe their leaders haven't got a clue about what is going on at the front line, they are hardly likely to be willing to follow them in a new direction.

It is hard for leaders to let go of the detail, particularly when they have to embody their organizations' styles, but if they cannot step back from the action today, the action tomorrow will not be appropriate or timely. Leaders have to be visionaries, with their feet firmly on the ground – dreamers and doers at the same time.

In Chapter 8, Ready, Fire, Aim, the focus switches from general goals to particular targets. The difference between a gun and a guided missile is instructive. Guns are not much good with moving targets, and most worthwhile targets are moving these days. Leaders need to develop action-oriented cultures, because when the targets are moving and are only in range for a moment, speed is more important than direction. The trick is to fire your missiles quickly, in roughly the right direction, and then rely on in-course corrections to zero in on the goal. In a fast-moving world, the market will probably have changed by the time your plans have come to fruition, so take action early and modify your plans as you go. This trial-and-error approach should be applied to every kind of action, from strategy formulation and marketing, to purchasing and selling.

That is why weak signal detection is so important. You need to spot threats and opportunities early so you can act early. You need to keep alert so you can detect subsequent weak signals that change the picture. And you need to maintain enough in-course flexibility to be able to adapt your action plans immediately, in the light of new information.

Chapter 9, Dogged Pursuit (and Knowing When to Stop), explores the fine line between doggedness and stubbornness. There is always a limit to how much energy the organization can muster at any one time, and leaders are effectively directing that energy when they identify priorities. The dilemma here is that organizational energy is precious, and may be squandered if its momentum is not sustained, but flexibility of approach is just as precious. Leaders must be dogged in pursuit of their priorities, without damaging their organizations' responsiveness to change.

The trick is to understand what is worth pursuing through thick and thin. Projects and change programmes should be ruthlessly evaluated and cut unless they prove sufficient value in support of the organization's purpose and visionary goals. Establish fixed, measurable goals, general enough to remain appropriate for the foreseeable future, and keep expressing and pursuing them in various ways until they are achieved. A goal must be general if it is to be durable, but it must also be clear, and progress towards it must be measurable if it is to gather sufficient momentum.

The final chapter summarizes the ideas and prescriptions set out in the three, central parts of the book, and describes how the interactions between them comprise a new model of leadership for the 21st century.

That is the plan of the book, but feel free to start wherever you like, and dip in and out of whatever parts or chapters catch your fancy. Each chapter is self-sufficient, in the sense that it includes its own set of principles illustrated by stories and anecdotes, and its own set of tools designed to help you implement the principles.

No two leaders face the same set of challenges, and even if they did, there is no reason to suppose the same solutions would be appropriate for both of them. We live in an equivocal world, with complex people who see things differently from us. But this does not mean that the sharing of experiences and the search for common themes and rhythms are fruitless.

The Alpha Leadership model we describe in the following pages is not a cookie-cutter version of reality that will work in all circumstances, for all people. Instead, we have tried to pull together, from our combined observations of what has worked for other leaders, a set of tips, clues and hints that may work for you.

We will often appear to contradict ourselves. We will urge you to build in redundancy, for example, *and* stretch resources; be agile beyond boundaries, *and* recognize your boundary constraints. The issues we are exploring with you here are not simple ones. As quantum physicist Nils Bohr put it: 'There are two types of truth. In a superficial truth, the opposite is false. In a deep truth, the opposite is also true.'

If, by sharing these ideas and approaches with you, we can help you to be more successful, to relieve some of the pressures of work and rediscover its joys, we will have succeeded in our aim.

References

1. *Management Today* (2000) Work/life balance survey, August.
2. Roberts, M. (1996) *The Man Who Listens to Horses*, Hutchinson.
3. Fox, E.M. and Urwick, L. (eds) (1973) *Dynamic Administration: the Collected Papers of Mary Parker Follett*, Pitman Publishing.

Part I

Anticipate

The dials on our economic dashboard have started spinning wildly, blinking and twittering as we head into new territory. It's possible the gauges are all broken, but it is much more likely that the world is turning upside down.

Kevin Kelly

In today's volatile world, the ability to anticipate is key. Technologies evolve at exponential rates. George Gilder forecasts that the total bandwidth of our communication systems will triple every 12 months for the foreseeable future;[1] computer systems that take 36 months to fully implement become obsolete in less than 18.

Our economies are increasingly based on intangible, ephemeral, knowledge assets – even the stalwart product of the industrial age, the car, has been described as a 'chip on wheels'.

The people in our organizations leave after shorter and shorter periods of employment. In 1989, executives averaged 2.9 employers in their career; in just 10 years this average increased to 5.2.[2] Of a sample of high fliers under the age of 37, 40% expected to leave their organizations in less than two years; only 7% anticipated staying longer than five.[3]

Coupled with these tectonic shifts is a disturbing trend in pricing. As Kevin Kelly, editor of *Wired*, puts it, the digital economy is moving all products and services towards higher quality at lower prices: 'a one-way trip over the cliff of inverted pricing and down the curve towards the free'.[4] Anticipation is a critical skill in today's business leaders – getting ahead of this curve is not just about turning a larger profit, it is key to an organization's survival.

Anticipation is *not* prediction. Those who claim to predict say that they can foresee the future, that they are sure what is going to happen. To anticipate is 'to expect . . . to deal with in advance . . . to realize beforehand . . . to bring on sooner'.[5] We believe that the future is essentially unpredictable, but that, nevertheless, through careful preparation and by staying alert, business leaders can 'realize beforehand'. Anticipation is about being on one's toes, ready to deal with whatever the future brings.

Organizations that can anticipate have three distinctive qualities: sensory systems that can detect important trends early; leaders whose minds are agile enough to spot the opportunities and threats embedded in them; and resources that are mobile enough to allow the organization to seize the opportunities and evade the threats in good time.

We will describe these three attributes in the following chapters. At the end of each chapter, we will provide you with some tools to help you improve your powers of anticipation.

As a business leader, well-honed skills in anticipation will help you to get ahead of the curve, increasing your chances of spotting business opportunities and exploiting them successfully. They will also increase your feeling of being in control, and reduce your feelings of stress when the unexpected happens – as it surely will. As Margaret Wheatley quotes, 'penetrating so many secrets, we cease to believe in the unknowable. But there it sits nevertheless, calmly licking its chops.'[6]

References

1. Gilder, G. (1997) 'Fiber keeps its promise: get ready'. *Forbes*, April 7.
2. Survey (1998) The war for talent, *McKinsey Quarterly*, 3.
3. Career Innovation Research Group (1999) Survey of high potentials from 73 countries.
4. Kelly, K. (1997) New Rules for the New Economy: Twelve dependable principles for thriving in a turbulent world, *Wired*, September.
5. *Chambers English Dictionary* (1988) Chambers and Cambridge University Press.
6. Menchen, quoted by Wheatley, M. (1999) *Leadership and the New Science*, Berrett-Koehler.

1

Detecting Weak Signals

Wealth is not gained by perfecting the known,
but by imperfectly seizing the unknown

Kevin Kelly

Anticipation starts with detecting weak signals. Everyone can hear a shout, but only those with exceptional sensory systems can hear the barely audible whispers where most of the opportunities and timely warnings lie.

You can only keep your organization on the leading edge of major trends if you can detect signals early, *before* they become clear. Messages that are so faint that they are inaudible to your rivals, and so equivocal as to be indistinguishable from 'white noise' to the average sensing system, must be your stock-in-trade, because by the time opportunities or threats become strong and clear, it may be too late to exploit or evade them.

We believe that, as business leaders, we can learn a lot about weak signal detection from two other species: frogs and bats. We draw conclusions from the limitations of the frog's sensory system and the sophistication of the bat's, and apply these conclusions to highlight the anticipation skills you need to succeed.

If your organization is more frog than bat, perhaps you need to change it.

Frogs recognize patterns

Put a frog in a glass jar with some recently expired flies and it will die of starvation. The frog can't see the fresh meat that surrounds it, because its sensory system was not 'designed' to spot motionless objects. Frogs see prey and predators with four sensors. One detects the contrast between the body of an object and its background, another perceives the object's curved shape, a third spots movements of curved shapes and a fourth senses changes in ambient light caused by movements of prey and predators.[1]

Once this information has been gathered, a pattern recognition circuit puts the four types of signal – contrast, shape, movement, light – together, and 'bleep', the frog recognizes the object as edible or dangerous, and either grabs it or leaps for safety. The important point here is that each type of sensor plays a vital part in bug detection. Still, curved objects, such as dead flies, do not compute.

Bats process signals

In his book, *The Blind Watchmaker*, evolutionist Richard Dawkins says that a bat's ultrasound sensory system achieves 'feats of detection and navigation that would strike an engineer dumb with admiration'.[2]

When cruising, the bat is content with a low frequency, stroboscopic view of its environment, and updates its picture of the night world with 10 pulses a second. When it detects prey, rivals or obstacles, however, the sonar pulse rate instantly soars to 200 a second – twice the speed at which fluorescent lights flicker.

A technical difficulty in echo systems is that the echo is much weaker than the original signal. If the system is to work over any distance, therefore, its transmitter (voice) must be very powerful and its receivers (ears) must be very sensitive. But powerful voices hurt sensitive ears. The solution is to switch ears off, during transmission, and then on again, in time for the echo. Some bats switch their ears off and on 50 times a second.

Bats also use frequency modulation to help them distinguish between outward pulses and inward echoes. Their brains can deduce the relative speeds and flight paths of their prey from the Doppler shift of returning echoes.

But why should we care about these differences between frogs and bats? Both species have survived the harsh tests of natural selection with their very different sensory systems.

The important comparison is not what the two systems have done for their respective species, but what they do for the *individuals*. Frogs live for two to three years, but some bats live for up to 50 years – much longer than any other rodent. The bat's sensory system helps to keep it alive and flying for decades, and this link between the sophistication of the sensory system and individual longevity applies to organizations, too.

Understanding sensory advantage

Every leader knows the value of sensing systems that 'keep tabs' on competitors, customers and emerging technologies. They are vital because anything a customer or competitor does could be a signal that demands a swift response, and emerging technologies can presage new markets and new commercial opportunities. But it is one thing to acknowledge the need for such a system, and quite another to design and build one.

What sort of things should it look for? How should it interpret signals and assign weights to them? What should be the status in the wider organization of those who run the system and analyse its output? What new skills must be learned and what old skills must be unlearned to ensure the system delivers a significant competitive advantage?

Multiplex scanning

Frogs and bats both have multiplex sensory systems, designed to receive and process several different kinds of signal, and both deduce meaning from the combination of the different signal types. They do not build a picture of prey or predator from one signal alone. One type of signal can trigger a reflex, but to stimulate intent it has to be corroborated by other signals.

Companies operating in competitive and fast-changing environments must also develop multiplex sensing systems, if they are not to be caught unawares by opportunities and threats. IBM lost its early dominance of the PC market because its scanning systems were not programmed to detect the kind of threat it was vanquished by. Back in those days, big companies assumed that the only serious threats to their market positions would come from similar organizations, and that threatening intent would always be clearly evident. IBM could 'see' Compaq, Dell, Intel and Microsoft, but its sensory system was not programmed to interpret their combined activities as threatening. IBM must have heard Bill Gates declare 'We set the standards', but paid no attention to him, just as a frog thinks nothing of bug-like shapes that don't move.

Organizations need 'always on' sensory systems constantly scanning for many different kinds of signal, and must be able to analyse the data received in sophisticated ways. Even with the help of the Hubble space telescope, modern astronomers can't see a planet orbiting a distant star, but they can deduce its presence from tiny anomalies in the star's movement. NATO forces in the Balkans could not see safe paths through minefields, but by emulating the bat, and listening very intently, under cover of darkness, to the footsteps of the minelayers, they could deduce them.

Multiplex sensing systems are invaluable in a business because the really important signals (those that, when acted on, confer competitive advantage) are usually ambiguous, often very weak, and may come from unexpected sources and directions.

The bat is hungrier for and much better at handling a range of signals. Its low cruising pulse rate can scan a wide area, with minimum energy, but when it gets an echo it can switch to higher frequency pulses, to gather as much information about its supposed prey as possible. Bats cannot see well, but they can hear the faintest of echoes and have built around their acute hearing a sensing system that has helped them become clinically efficient predators. Organizations should also be able to switch their sensory systems between a low-resolution, scanning mode, and a high-resolution, information-gathering mode.

The scope of your sensing mechanisms should be carefully thought through in relation to your organization's purpose and vision. Weak signal mechanisms need to incorporate anything that might have impact on your purpose now and in the future. Mechanisms need to focus on the core business, but also recognize that important whispers may emanate from the periphery of today's business rather than its centre. For example, scanning in the light-fittings business should enable detection of signals both within the fittings industry, and also from advances and trends within enabling technologies such as plastics and electronics.

Organizations must gather, and make sense of, the widest possible range of information because you never know where the next threat will come from, or what form it will take.

Handling ambiguity: recognizing patterns in weak signals

The bat's sensory system is programmed for 'weak signal detection' because the winners in the night war are those who spot predators and prey early. A sophisticated, broad-ranging sensory system is not much use if competitors with less sophisticated systems can spot prey before you. It is the same in business. An organization's sensing system will only give it a real edge if it can detect signals before they become clear and unambiguous.

This is a problem for business because, like a whisper, a weak signal may be ambiguous. There may be other signals that contradict it, its weakness may make it hard to understand, or may simply mean it signifies nothing. It may be tantalizingly equivocal, but it must not be ignored because, if you wait until things become clear before you act, you will act too late.

The frog's 'grab it' reflex is only triggered if all four of its signal types light up. A light for a fly shape is a necessary, but not a sufficient stimulus. Frogs respond with astonishing speed to an unambiguous signal set (four lights), but don't respond at all to an ambiguous signal set (between one and three lights), and they miss some easy meals as a consequence.

If interest-rate-fixing bodies, such as America's Federal Reserve Board and the European Central Bank, used signal sensing and processing systems like the frog's, they would have no chance of controlling inflation. As a former central bank deputy governor pointed out, those who urge rate-fixing bodies not to change rates until the need for a change is clear, fail to grasp the essence of a central bank's role. 'If . . . [they] changed rates only when the evidence was clear . . . [they] would always be changing them too late . . . Unclear evidence should be . . . [their] stock-in-trade'.[3]

Interest-rate-setting institutions can only maintain the economies in their care in the virtuous zone, where economic growth is just a little lower than the rate at which inflation starts to accelerate, if they react to the weak signals that precede the strong.

An ability to detect and analyse weak signals is essential when markets are absorbing disruptive technologies, such as the Internet and third generation wireless telecommunications technologies (3G), because the adoption of such dynamic technologies often generates phase transitions and exponential growth curves. Bob Metcalfe, inventor of the Ethernet, gave his name to a law of networks by pointing out that network value increases geometrically with size – a two-node network makes one connection, a three-node network makes three, four nodes make six, and so on. 'Metcalfe's Law' means nascent trends can explode into major phenomena overnight.

Kevin Kelly tells the tale of a lily leaf on a pond which begins as a single cell, and doubles in size each day. A week before it covers the whole pond, it covers less than 1% of the pond. In other words, it is critical to spot an important innovation before it takes off, before it passes our usual threshold of attention. In the network economy, this is more critical than ever before because 'smaller initial pools can lead to runaway dominance'.[4]

One of the least commented on, but most important, tasks of today's business leaders is to equip their organizations with sensing systems that can spot the early stages of such exponential growth explosions. We will describe how leaders can prepare their organizations to react quickly to such signals in Chapters 3 and 6. Our point here is that if you don't spot them early, you can't reap the benefit.

Shutting out the white noise

The difficulty with systems sensitive enough to detect weak signals is that they can be damaged by local noise. For an interest-rate-setting body, such as the US Federal Reserve Board, the local noise is the clamour of lobbyists urging it not to change rates too soon. For a bat, it is the loud pulses it must transmit if it is to get audible echoes from distant objects. The bat solves the problem by switching its ears off and on. The 'Fed' solves the problem in much the same way – by turning a deaf ear to lobbyists with axes to grind, and listening intently for weaker messages from neutral sources.

In most organizations the inside noise is so loud and so incessant that the whisperings and rustlings outside that indicate opportunities and threats are often inaudible. Important components of this deafening, internal noise are the assumptions and mental models that become embedded in the cognitive processes with which organizations filter and make sense of the information they receive.

When a lone CIA agent told America's State Department that the Soviet Union was shipping missile parts to Cuba, officials ignored the report because it was inconsistent with their belief that Soviet President Khrushchev had no hostile intent. When the Thiokol engineer, Roger Boisjoly, warned NASA that Thiokol O-ring seals on the *Challenger* space shuttle's solid rocket motors could fail if the shuttle was launched on a cold day, his memo was ignored because, as Boisjoly later told a Presidential Commission on the *Challenger* disaster: 'I felt personally that management was under a lot of pressure to launch.'

The record shows that similar early warnings were issued and ignored before the airborne raid on Arnhem at the end of the Second World War, before the *Herald of Free Enterprise* ferry disaster in March 1987 and before flight TE 901, carrying 257 people, crashed in broad daylight into the active volcano, Mt Erebus in Antarctica, in November 1979. In each case new knowledge, in the form of warnings, challenged conventional wisdom and was rejected, much as a body's immune system attacks and attempts to eject 'foreign' organisms.

In a similar way, your own price list could be blocking your organization's ability to 'hear' its market. Companies put a lot of thought into their pricing strategies, and price lists are generally regarded as vital inputs for cashflow planning and investment appraisal. They are convenient, certainly, but with the advent of Internet auctions, are they still realistic? 'What's the list price of my company's stock?' asked Sun Microsystems CEO Scott McNealy. 'There is none; there's a market. So why is there a list price for your products? There shouldn't be; there should be a market.'[5] Sun uses Internet auctions, partly because a price list can become obsolete before it is printed, but mostly because they give Sun a much better market feel.

Knowledge is in the mind of the knower. As Alfred Korzybski points out, 'the map is not the territory'.[6] A map is data about a territory, not a 100% accurate depiction of the territory itself. In the same way, our knowledge about an event or situation is carefully selected in support of our hypotheses. It is frequently 'political' in the sense that vested interests adhere to one version or another, irrespective of its intrinsic merits. These days, we have come to regard knowledge as the most precious of all business assets, but with assets like these, who needs liabilities?

The huge organizations that dominate our business landscape are products of an evolutionary process that has insulated them from the outside world. In the late 19th century, when they first emerged, their competitive advantage was their ability to coordinate business processes better than the market. They became very good coordinators and managers but, in the process, they lost the habits of watching and listening, and their sensory systems atrophied.

Now that markets have become more efficient, these large organizations have lost their coordinating edge. They must relearn the sensing art, and reinvent the sensing systems that smaller, more market-oriented firms never lost. To do this they will need to unlearn the habits and review the tacit assumptions that have deadened their senses.

Building sensory advantage

Lepers do not lose fingers and limbs because their fingers and limbs become diseased. They lose them because their central nervous systems are damaged in a way that prevents them from feeling pain and thus avoiding injuries to their extremities. Consequently, parts of fingers and other extremities can be damaged and even torn off without the leper feeling anything. Long ago, when many lepers were forced to live in caves, the rest of the population thought the disease destroyed fingers. Actually, while the lepers slept, cave-dwelling rats would eat their fingers. And the lepers did not have the blessing or gift of pain to signal the need to move their hands out of danger.

An organization that loses touch with its 'skin' risks a similar kind of injury. It is often said that one of the advantages large companies have over small companies is that they have more 'skin', in the form of much larger numbers of customer-facing staff. But it is not enough to be bristling with external sensors. Firms have to use their customer-facing people as sensors, because if they are not used for sensing, they become desensitized like the extremities of the leper.

The grocery retailing industry is a case in point. It has performed well in recent years, but it is now struggling with increasingly well-informed, but more time-constrained customers, tougher competition, longer opening hours and demand for higher quality at lower prices.

Rather than use their customer-facing people as sensors, senior retail managers at central headquarters often become disconnected from the 'skin' of their local stores. The centre tries to improve consistency, by issuing a series of 'flavours of the month' priorities, focusing its attention on availability, staff costs, scheduling and so on, and loses touch with local environments. In fact, scheduling may not be a problem at all at a particular store. The issue may be poor management that makes staff unwilling to put themselves out, local skill shortages or some other reason that has nothing to do with the scheduling system. If leaders at the centre were more sensitive to their local staff, who in turn are sensitive to the local customers and environment, they would be able to become aware of and respond to 'weak signals' much earlier.

We will devote the rest of this chapter to tools and techniques leaders may find helpful as they embark on the task of reestablishing contact with the skins of their organizations, and building and commissioning sensory systems sensitive and sophisticated enough to enable them to anticipate events.

Tools for thought

1. Skin-driven management

Strategic planning does not work as well as it used to. Over the past decade or so, more and more painstakingly developed strategies have been overtaken by events and shelved. We assume that the problem lies in the planning process, and try to modernize it by improving communications between planners and doers and reducing planning cycles. But the problem is not the process. It is the whole idea of strategic planning in turbulent business environments.

When the rate of external change is low, strategic planning works well, but once the rate of change exceeds a critical level, clarity and precision are less valuable than agility, and strategic plans can become liabilities. But if companies operating in volatile environments should not be guided by strategy, what should they be guided by? Our answer is that their 'skin' should guide them: by the signals, weak and strong, that market-facing staff are constantly receiving. Actions should 'emerge' from market contact directly, without rerouting through the centre.

Most companies employ strategy formulation processes that are 'emergent' to an extent. To handle faster change, they have decentralized decision making and given those closest to the customer more voice. This has been done in a piecemeal way, however, by adding dotted line relationships to the central planning system. There has been input from beyond the centre, but no formal contribution.

Input is not enough. A company cannot anticipate events without a guidance system driven rather than merely influenced by messages from its skin. The successful companies of the future will be those with the best skin-driven planning systems, not those with the best plans.

How should a leader go about reconnecting the organization with its skin?

In *Every Business is a Growth Business*, Ram Charan and Noel Tichy describe how Wal-Mart has arranged real-time feeds of weak signals into its purchasing. From Monday to Wednesday each week, regional managers visit Wal-Mart's and competitors' stores. They interview store staff, their customers and their competitors' customers, look at prices and ranges, and watch for shifts in buying patterns, merchandising and promotions. On Thursdays, they return to Wal-Mart's Bentonville headquarters, report their findings at a top-level meeting with advertising, logistics and merchandise managers, and buying, merchandising, pricing and promotions decisions are taken there and then.[7]

Other examples of such 'social operating mechanisms' cited by Charan and Tichy are General Electric Medical Systems' 'Quick Market Intelligence' system, where regional and business bosses share market intelligence every week; Compaq's 'Innovate Forum', where executives discuss ideas with customers and business partners; GE Capital's strategic planning process, which begins with brainstorming sessions for which no preparation is allowed, and AlliedSignal's new product development process, which reviews each project monthly and will not sanction any project with a time-to-launch of more than 20 months.

Charan later identified six key features of 'social operating mechanisms':

- The process feeds real-time information into the organization.
- It relies on external, rather than internal, data.
- It fosters dialogue.
- It generates complete pictures of the market, across all dimensions (supply chain, customers, competitors, employees).
- The information gathered is fed directly into key decision-making processes and incorporates follow-through action.
- The process is rhythmic and repeats over short cycles.

Of course, real-time, skin-driven operating mechanisms of this kind, that allow action to follow swiftly on the heels of signal detection, require a macrocontext in the form of more general, less frequently gathered information. It would be crazy, for instance, to take decisions on the basis of a sudden increase in demand for a particular product, without taking into account the impact of the impending introduction of a new tax. Operating mechanisms themselves will generate information about trends that may only make sense in terms of slower, deeper economic and cultural rhythms.

The following tools will help leaders to reestablish contact with the skins of their organizations, and to build sensory systems which will enhance their ability to anticipate events.

1.1 Building skin-driven management processes

Identify where market insights will have most impact on your business. Work through the following checklist to construct a skin-driven process.

1. Who has market knowledge? Who else needs to know it?
2. What is the best mechanism for sharing this knowledge?
   - Face to face? E-mail? Teleconference?
   - How frequently should knowledge sharing occur?
3. How can you ensure that everyone participates every time?
   - Feedback mechanisms?
   - Relevance checks?
   - Peer pressure?
   - Formal performance measurement?
4. What skills do participants need to ensure the process is a dialogue rather than a series of monologues? How do you encourage people to acquire these skills?
5. How can you ensure that the information is acted on?
   - What could get in the way?
   - What can you do to remove these obstacles?
   - How do you ensure sufficient visibility of the process to underpin its effectiveness?

This exercise can easily be adapted for leaders who have responsibility for departments whose customers are inside the business rather than outside it. Finance departments, corporate services, product development, HR, training and development, IT and other back-office functions would be more effective if they were more responsive to their internal customers. At a time when organizations are focusing on their 'cores' and brand identities, and outsourcing other functions, you cannot assume your internal customers will always be captive. At some point they will claim the right to exercise choice in the supplier of the service you provide. You can only prepare for that by becoming skin-driven yourself.

1.2 Hearing the unexpected

It is always easier to hear what you expect to hear – to absorb information that corroborates what you already believe. So how do we avoid the business equivalent of the *Challenger* disaster?

There are simple phrases you can practise using or avoiding when processing information that does not fit with your view of the world – which is likely to happen quite often when you are adopting a skin-driven management process for the first time.

When you next hear something you did not expect or do not believe, try the phrases shown in Table 1.1.

Table 1.1 *Hearing the unexpected*

Say more of . . .	Say less of . . .
So you think [*summarize back to them their last statement*]. Tell me more . . .	No, that won't work, because . . .
That's interesting, tell me more . . .	No that's wrong . . . you know that . . .
I didn't think that was the case. Why have things changed?	We already looked at that . . .
That data surprises me. What does it mean?	The numbers must be wrong . . .
That's interesting, how did you come up with the data?	Who put those figures together? [*smirk or negative tone of voice to discount the source*]
John, this is obviously important to you . . . take me through it again telling me what is the basis of your point of view . . .	John's on his hobby horse again [*cue for everyone to laugh*]
John, you often see things from a different angle. You may have a point. What is making you think the consensus view is wrong?	John, how come you never support the consensus view around here?

2. Pattern recognition

You and your fellow directors are seated at a table in a wood-panelled room at your investment bankers. The atmosphere is electric. One of your closest competitors has just outbid you for another company and you have to decide whether to bid more or drop out of the auction. You know your CEO (a friend as well as a boss) is up for it. You have never seen him so enthused. He is loving it. He has had more press in the past three weeks than in the previous five years. He is being described as a visionary. It's a feeling you share of reshaping the industry, of being agents of history.

Your investment bankers have rerun the numbers, and they show you can go a little higher, but you are worried. You felt OK about the first bid, but the new offer seems too high. How can you tell him? He will just refer you to the new numbers, urge you to 'dare to be great' and tell you that this is a strategic acquisition.

You shouldn't have to play the 'party-pooper'. Your friend, the CEO, should be able to read your body language. When, against your better judgement, you eventually agree to the higher offer, he should be watching you closely for any sign that you are acting as a friend, rather than a responsible CFO. He knows you well. He should be able to detect the pattern of 'no' behind your voiced 'yes'; to read, in your body language, your fear that he is about to fall victim to 'the winner's curse' of auction theory.

When Charles Matthews was appointed managing director of operations at Rolls-Royce Motors, he found himself at the pinnacle of a reporting hierarchy that began on the shopfloor, and moved up through team leaders, zone managers, senior production managers and thence to the manufacturing director. By the time information reached him, it had been heavily filtered. His 'feel' was blunted by distance.

So Matthews took to walking around the factory with his coach, honing his listening and watching skills. He learned how to make shopfloor staff feel at ease with him, how to read non-verbal signals, and how to corroborate his understanding by saying: 'So your view is that . . .' Good listeners use such 'reflective listening' naturally, and everyone can do it with practice. He learned to assume there was something useful or important in everything he heard. On several occasions, staff subjected him to strong verbal attacks on issues close to their hearts. People knew they could talk to him because, even when he disagreed with, or did not act on, their input, he listened and responded. He was always trying to heighten his awareness.

Here are two tools you can use to heighten your awareness.

2.1 Reading behind the words

1. Attend a low-value meeting that you would not usually attend, because its agenda is not sufficiently close to your key objectives.
2. Sit where you can easily see everyone else.
3. Study the body language without interpreting it and try to ignore the verbal content. Do not assume non-verbal messages 'mean' anything in particular. Some generalizations may be possible, but go easy on your interpretations, because they may be wrong.
4. Once you have watched for a while, 'turn up the volume' on the words a little and, still concentrating on the body language, try to identify

when the speaker's non-verbal messages seem to support and contradict what they are saying.

Body language supports verbal messages when:
- there is some 'congruence' between the two languages: when, for instance, the speaker smiles when talking about good things and frowns when talking about problems;
- the speaker's seating position is symmetrical – feet in similar positions; arms, hands and head balanced, etc.;
- the tempo of voice is regular.

Body language contradicts verbal messages when:
- a speaker seems to lack confidence in what he or she is saying;
- body posture is asymmetrical;
- movements are jerky;
- the emotion conveyed seems to deny the words uttered.

5. When you spot a contradiction between the verbal and non-verbal, step into the speaker's shoes and try to guess what it means. It might be about himself or herself as a person, or his or her confidence in the matters being discussed.

6. Check your guess at the time if appropriate, or after the meeting. Be careful how you put it. If you say 'I was watching you and your body language suggested you don't believe what you were saying', he or she may be offended. Be more subtle: 'I was thinking about [*the issue at hand*], and wondered if we had thought enough about . . . [*what you think the non-verbal signal meant*].'

2.2 Multiplying the perspectives

Economies, the markets for products and services, and the internal workings of organizations are complex systems driven by positive feedback loops, and their behaviour is therefore very hard to predict. One way of managing the unpredictability of complex systems is to look at them from many different angles. The more points of view you take, and the more signals you seek out, the more you can learn about a complex system's behaviour.

This technique will help to increase the sensitivity and widen the scope of your sensory system.

1. Draft a list of people including those senior, on the same level and junior to you in yours and other parts of the organization; radicals and

conservatives; those who do and do not share your views; insiders and outsiders, and people of all ethnic origins, including your own.

2. Approach everyone on the list; say why you want to talk to them, and book 45-minute interviews with each of them.

3. Begin the interview by telling the interviewee that you want to hear his or her views of the future to enrich your own views, and then ask the following questions:

- *Wonder*
  If a time traveller from 50 years in the future could give you the answer to one question, what would it be?

- *Pride*
  If you were looking back 10 years from now and telling the tale of the organization's greatest success, what would the story be and why?

- *Shame*
  If you were looking back 10 years from now and telling the tale of the organization's greatest failure, what would the story be and why?

- *Memory*
  What does the organization need to forget?
  What must it always remember?

- *Imperatives*
  What are the most important strategic decisions we will have to make as an organization?

- *Obstacles and dangers*
  What will prevent us from succeeding?
  What are the greatest risks and dangers?

- *Priorities*
  If you had the power to do one thing for the organization, what would it be, and why?

- *Closure*
  What should I have asked you that I didn't?

4. Having completed the interviews, review your data and create pictures based on strong and weak signals, and classify the scenarios according to whether you like or dislike them.

5. Review your learning. Are you any wiser, and if so, in what ways? Are there weak signals you should monitor? If so, how should you monitor

them, and how regularly? What worked in the interview process and what didn't? How would you improve it, and is the exercise worth repeating?

3. Signal processing

Students of the Japanese martial art, Aikido, learn to 'read' body language and other von-verbal messages to avoid fights, as well as to win them. When walking along a street, they are not lost in daydreams of life and love, or preoccupied with thoughts of work. Their senses are tuned to the here and now. They are 'aware', in a relaxed way, of people up to 100 yards ahead of them. If it is late and the area is rough, they notice drunks outside bars, loiterers and the 'vibes' emanating from individuals or small groups. They are very sensitive to sounds, and after years of training in noisy, crowded martial arts studios, they become acutely aware of what is happening around them.

They learn to transmit as well as to receive non-verbal signals. Two Aikido students were standing outside a restaurant in a deserted part of town when a small group of young men approached them closely, as if to surround them. Both martial artists imperceptibly readied themselves. One identified the group's leader, made eye contact with him and smiled, letting him know that he was aware of the situation. The leader caught the smile, smiled back and kept on walking, followed by his gang. On another occasion, a man crossed a street, and ran towards an Aikido student. The martial artist changed his posture very slightly (known as 'settling the hips') and the runner swerved to avoid him.

Aikido masters use their eyes and ears to read what's going on inside their opponents' heads, because they know that if they can see the intention that precedes the action, they will have a slight edge, and a slight edge may be all they need. Leaders who can read facial expressions and other non-verbal languages, and so anticipate how people will act, or read how they feel deep down about an instruction or a situation, also have an edge.

Loud signals tend to drown the weak, but Aikido masters know that volume is a bad guide to significance. If you focus intently on a weak signal, you may realize its intensity is increasing and about to reach a step change when it will become deafening.

3.1 Graphic equalizer exercise

Leaders must become the operators of a virtual equivalent of those 'graphic equalizers' the music buff tinkers with and forensic audio engineers use to analyse background noise in recorded sounds. To extract the maximum meaning from the information they receive, they must become adept at amplifying the weak and suppressing the strong signals. The following exercise can be done on your own, but is usually more fruitful with a small group.

1. Select up to six participants eager to experiment and explore ideas.
2. Select a subject area of mutual interest, about which strong, medium and weak signals are being received. Prepare three flip charts, one each for strong, medium and weak signals. Draw two columns on the right-hand side of each flip chart.
3. List signals, from inside and from outside the organization, on the left-hand side of each chart. Once you have listed the obvious strong signals, do some brainstorming to make sure that you list all the medium and weak signals. You may only become aware of some of the most interesting weak signals during this discussion. Try to find time, before the meeting, to generate a list of weak signals by doing the 'Multiplying the perspectives' exercise described above.
4. Review the lists. Make sure you have covered all the signals, and include repetitions when different words express differences in meaning that are important to individuals. Ensure all voices, not just the loudest, are heard.
5. Agree a signal strength score for each item: 10–7 for strong signals; 6–3 for medium; 0–2 for weak. Discuss your different perceptions, as you build a consensus on relative signal strengths. Write the scores in the first column on the charts.
6. Select three items from each list, the volumes of which the group thinks could usefully be altered to improve the balance of inputs to decision making. You might want to reduce the volumes of strong signals, increase the volumes of weak signals and adjust medium signals either way. Write the agreed alterations in the second column of the charts.

Volume changes should not be arbitrary. Discussions, and reaching consensus about assigning strength to particular signals, are an important part of the exercise because they achieve buy-in from the group about how to implement next steps.

7. Take the nine signals (three from each list) whose volume you have decided to change and decide how to implement the changes.

Some ways to weaken strong signals:
- Stop inviting the sender of the signal to your meetings.
- Ask a member of your group to provide counter-examples, whenever the signal seems too intense.
- Interfere with the signal, by injecting 'noise', such as humour.
- If the signal comes from an external channel, such as a publication, find another external channel transmitting a different signal.
- If the strong message is the dominant consensus within your business, reduce its relative strength by increasing the intensity of medium and weak signals.

Some ways to strengthen weak signals:
- If the senders attend your meetings, strengthen their voices by:
  - giving them more speaking time;
  - forbidding interruptions;
  - asking them to expand on their views – 'reflective listening' is useful here – summarize what they have said using their words as much as possible and say, 'It would be good if you could tell us more about . . .' or 'Help me understand this better . . .', and then ask an open question (a 'how', 'what' or 'why' question, rather than a question that can be answered with a 'yes' or 'no');
  - encouraging them privately and publicly to be more vocal.
- If the signal is an external source, such as a publication reporting on a social trend, you could increase the signal strength by:
  - getting more sources;
  - spreading the message more widely in the organization;
  - finding ways to give key managers more exposure to the signal;
  - conduct research, to gather more data on the signal.
8. Agree to meet to review progress on next steps.
9. Spend a few moments discussing what you have learned that was useful and interesting, and how you could improve the learning next time.

3.2 Dialogue circles

The need to ensure meetings become arenas for dialogue rather than a series of monologues is well documented,[8] but can't be emphasized enough. Too often, the potential for rich information sharing in face-to-face meetings is squandered on power games and political manoeuvring. As Bill Isaacs of MIT says: 'In meetings we have two modes of being – speaking and waiting to speak'. We are so focused on our own contributions that we do not listen to others. In theory, meetings should be crescendos of rising understanding as each new contribution builds on the last. In practice, they tend to become staccato sequences of monologues, each of which is only loosely, if at all, connected to earlier comments. How often have you heard someone say exactly what you said five minutes earlier?

Such behaviour is natural, because people inevitably bring to meetings their own agendas, such as their desires to claim credit, avoid blame or impress peers and superiors. Because it is difficult to behave in a meeting in ways that foster information sharing, leaders may find it useful to impose rules on those attending. Isaacs has designed a process known as a 'dialogue circle', which can be particularly useful when the cause of a problem is unclear, and it is worth making sure you are asking the right questions.

- Assemble the 7–10 people most closely associated with the problem.
- Sit in a circle.
- Appoint one member as note taker.
- Tell everyone else to focus on what is said, without taking notes.
- Ask one person to state the question that he or she feels the team is there to resolve.
- Tell the next person to begin by saying what the first person's question means to him or her and what thoughts it provokes, and then to say what other *question* the first question has prompted in his or her mind.
- Resist all temptation to answer the question!

The point is to hold the space – to prevent people from going for the quick answer. The technique is designed to produce a multifaceted description of the problem, and explore its essence. Be ruthless with those who spend time planning their own questions, rather than listening to their colleagues and responding accordingly. (They're easy to spot. They're the ones who will be trying to answer someone else's question, or asking a question unrelated to that of the previous speaker!)

- Do two or three rounds of the circle.
- Ask the note taker to review the questions that have arisen.

- Reflect with the team on what this means for the problem-solving task.

For more resources on detecting weak signals, visit www.AlphaLeaders.com

Conclusion

There are many ways to increase our ability to detect weak signals relevant to the organizations we lead. The important point is that, unlike frogs and bats, which were endowed with their sensory systems by evolution, we have to design and construct business sensory systems deliberately. We have our senses, of course, and we can learn to use them better to read body language and other non-verbal signals, but to be able to *anticipate* rather than just *react* to events, leaders need more than their own senses.

Astronomers involved in SETI – the Search for Extraterrestrial Intelligence – can't rely on their own ears. They need hearing aids in the form of radio telescopes that they arrange in arrays called 'radio interferometers' that span the globe. Business leaders need to build something similar: a kind of cognitive prosthesis consisting of networks of listeners on watch for faint signals from many sources, and the ability to make sense of them.

We now turn in Chapter 2 to the qualities leaders need to turn such systems to their organizations' advantage.

References

1. Lettvin, J.Y., Maturana, H.R., McCulloch, W.S. and Pitts, W.H. (1965) What the frog's eye tells the frog's brain, *Embodiments of Mind*, The MIT Press.
2. Dawkins, R. (1986) *The Blind Watchmaker*, Longman.
3. Pennant-Rea, R. (2001) Ambiguity and interest rates, *The Financial Times*, 25 January.
4. Kelly, K. (1998) *New Rules for the New Economy*, Viking Penguin.
5. McNealy (2001) Welcome to the bazaar, *Harvard Business Review*, March.
6. Korzybski, A. (1980) *Science and Sanity*, The International Non-Aristotelian Library, Lakeville, CN.
7. Charan, R. and Tichy, N. (1998) *Every Business is a Growth Business*, Times Books.
8. Deering, A. and Murphy A. (1998) *See The Difference Engine*, Gower.

2

Developing Mental Agility

Imagination is more important than knowledge
Albert Einstein

On 18 November 1995, the violinist Itzhak Perlman performed at the Lincoln Center in New York City. He had polio as a child and walks with crutches. The audience waited patiently as he made his way slowly across the stage to his chair, sat down, put his crutches on the floor, removed the braces from his legs, settled himself in his characteristic pose, one foot tucked back, the other pushed forwards, bent down to pick up his violin, gripped it with his chin, and nodded to the conductor to indicate he was ready.

It was a familiar ritual for Perlman fans: the crippled genius making light of his disability before his sublime music transcended everything. But this time was different.

'Just as he finished the first few bars,' the *Houston Chronicle* music critic recalls, 'one of the strings on his violin broke. You could hear it snap – it went off like gunfire across the room. There was no mistaking what that sound meant. There was no mistaking what he had to do.' It was obvious – he had to put down his violin, replace his braces, pick up the crutches, heave himself to his feet, make his laborious way offstage and either get another violin or restring his crippled instrument.

He didn't. He closed his eyes for a moment, and then signalled the conductor to begin again. The audience was spell-bound.

Everyone knows it is impossible to play a symphonic work with just three strings. I know that, and you know that, but that night Itzhak Perlman refused to know that. He played with such passion and such power and such purity . . . You could see him modulating, changing, and recomposing the piece in his

head . . . At one point it sounded like he was de-tuning the strings to get . . .
sounds from them they had never made before.'

When he finished there was an awed silence, and then the audience rose,
as one.

We were all on our feet, screaming and cheering – doing everything we could
to show him how much we appreciated what he'd done. He smiled, wiped the
sweat from his brow, raised his bow to quiet us, and then he said, not
boastfully, but in a quiet, pensive, reverent tone, 'You know, sometimes it is the
artist's task to find out how much music he can still make with what he
has left'.[1]

Variations on an agile theme

Agile is not an adjective that springs readily to mind when watching Itzhak
Perlman walking, but for those who saw him that night at the Lincoln
Center it was entirely appropriate. It was not just the nimbleness of his fingers that awed them, it was also the agility of his mind. He had a job to do
and on that occasion he had to do it with a crippled instrument. Perhaps it
was his life-long experience with a crippled body that led him to reject the
conventional solution to a broken violin and try instead to get three strings
to do the work of four.

Strings break, circumstances change, but life goes on. In the business world
too, leaders need to be mentally agile. They need skills in the three vital
characteristics of mental agility: exploring beyond their boundaries, recognizing the limits within which creativity operates successfully, and being flexible in pursuit of goals despite encountering obstacles to their achievement.

Agile leaders don't keep their mental agility in reserve for when things go
wrong. They use it to respond to the threats and opportunities they detect
in the 'weak signals' they receive through their multiplex sensing systems.
Their minds are constantly seeking new ways to exploit their own and their
organizations' distinctive abilities. Steven Spielberg didn't stop at reinvent-
ing the thriller, with *Duel*. He has applied his film-making genius throughout his career to the invention and reinvention of genres with such
pioneering blockbusters as *Jaws*, *Indiana Jones*, *Schindler's List* and *Saving
Private Ryan*.

But agile leaders are not wildly, or chaotically, creative. Spielberg is flexible within the limits of the cinematic industry. Effective agility generates a

variety of responses proportional to the variety in their environments. Perlman played the same piece to the same audience, but in a different way, to compensate for the near catastrophic change that had taken place in his equipment.

Agile leaders do not abandon their goals, just because their chosen routes cease to be available for one reason or another. They bob and weave, duck and dive, and seek other routes and means to achieve their objectives. And if they can't find any, or can't find any in time, they modify or change their goals to bring them within reach.

We live in the natural world, but also in a world we have imagined and made real. The words, grammar, ideas, ink, paper and printing press of which and with which this book has been made, the music Perlman played, from the films and theme parks of Spielberg and Disney, to the advances of biotechnology, all were, at one time, dreams that human energy has realized. And this world we build with our imaginations is a work in progress – each moment of each day more dream stuff is turned into reality.

This constant process of dream realization is manifested not only in rapid technological advance and endless streams of new products and services, but also in changing tastes, outlooks and behaviours, as people imagine and then experiment with new styles of living. The world is not in equilibrium, and never will be. It is constantly changing, and those who make their living from meeting the needs of its inhabitants must be consistently agile in response. To prosper, they must innovate constantly.

It is often said, 'If you always do what you have always done, you will always get what you always got.' This is quite wrong. If you always do what you have always done, someone else will eat your lunch.

Beyond boundaries

Gregory Bateson defines wisdom as the recognition that we are all part of a system.[2] Systems maintain their balance through highly complex, interactive feedback loops, which make it impossible to predict what will happen next through a linear, $a + b = c$ type of analysis. The only way to increase our ability to predict what will happen next in a system is therefore to view that system from multiple and diverse points of view. In Chapter 1 we described ways to create diversity in the signals we use to manage our businesses. The next step is to develop the skills to handle those messages appropriately: to take on board something new rather than block it; to see opportunity in feedback that contradicts your view of the world rather than to deny its veracity; to seek opportunities to apply your core skills in other markets – in other words, to move beyond your boundaries.

The commercial prize available to those organizations gifted in this kind of exploration is clear. One example is the development of the photocopier. Chester Carlson, inventor of the first dry copier, researched optics technology back to the Ancient Greeks, transcending his boundaries of time and place in order to develop a breakthrough technology. Decades later, Canon looked outside their heartland photographic markets to the burgeoning copier industry, and stole it from its original inventors.

So how do you promote your own and your organization's ability to explore beyond its boundaries? There are two keys: ensure sufficient variety and generate multiple interpretations of incoming signals.

Variety, the spice of life

Ashby's *Law of Requisite Variety*[3] states that 'only variety can absorb variety', and that a regulating system must be able to generate as many states as the variety of the system being regulated. Put simply, it means that organizations will only succeed if they can generate as much internal variety as the variety surrounding them externally. In other words, their resources must be at least as diverse as their volatile marketplaces.

History provides us with numerous lessons in the importance of variety. Some scientists believe Cro-Magnon man vanquished the first species of *Homo sapiens*, the Neanderthals, roughly 50 000 years ago, not because they were smarter, but because they had more fertile imaginations. Neanderthals first appeared during the Ice Age. Their brains were a little larger than our's and Cro-Magnon man's, but were located a little lower down in the skull. It seems that the elevation of the Cro-Magnon brain left room for the evolution of a larger palate, which made speech more precise, and so led to the development of language.

Language fired the Cro-Magnons' imagination. They dreamt of and made better clothing, shelter and tools than the Neanderthals, and learned how to plan, organize and cooperate more efficiently. There is a sameness about all the Neanderthal sites that have been excavated: the same simple hand-held stone tools, the same wooden thrusting spears, and no art. Cro-Magnon excavations have revealed not only more sophistication, but also more diversity – tools of bone as well as stone, compound artefacts, such as bows and arrows, nets made of rope, jewellery and wonderful cave paintings.

Greater behavioural variety enabled the Cro-Magnons to adapt more successfully to their environment and to displace their equally smart, but less imaginative, Neanderthal competitors.

An ability to assume many states, dream of many possibilities, imagine many devices, conceive of many processes, foresee many opportunities and prepare for many contingencies is as important in social as in evolutionary systems. Potatoes were grown throughout Europe in the 19th century as a staple food, but the effect of the potato blights in 1845 and 1846 was devastating in Ireland because Irish farmers grew practically nothing else. The potato had become *the* staple crop in Ireland, rather than one of several staples, because it was easy to grow, thrived in Irish soil and offered much higher yields per acre than wheat. The Irish people were totally dependent on the potato crop and when it failed for two years, millions died of starvation, fell victim to dysentery, cholera, scurvy or typhus, or emigrated. Between 1851 and 1946 three and a half million Irish people left Ireland for America.

The effect of the potato blight was harsh, but not as devastating elsewhere in Europe, because wheat had remained a staple. Ireland's food chain lacked sufficient variety, and had been a catastrophe waiting to happen ever since the potato became the Irish 'monoculture' in the 19th century.

It is not a matter of competing with or controlling a changing system. It is a matter of embracing, rather than running from the variety, of growing and evolving with the system's burgeoning complexity, rather than attempting to recapture its earlier simplicity.

In the late 1970s and early 1980s, inventors at Xerox Corporation's Palo Alto Research Center (PARC) linked the 'mouse' pointing device, developed at the Stanford Research Institute, to a 'graphical user interface' (GUI). Although these two technologies were the keys that would unlock the mass market for the personal computer (PC), they created little value for Xerox whose entry into the PC market with its Star computer in 1981 was late, misconceived and short-lived.

Xerox at that time was not the kind of company to make best use of the mental agility of the young, talented free-thinkers assembled at PARC. Despite enjoying the early fruits of their diversity, the corporation expected these inventors to conform to the strictures of corporate life. Xerox lacked the agility to exploit the new market and, as a corporation, couldn't accommodate the culture of PARC. Contrast this outcome with Steve Job's approach, who tempted PARC scientists over to Apple with the promise: 'You don't need to change, we will build a company around you.'

Apple arguably made the opposite mistake, when it 'closed' its architecture to preserve its lead in the GUI software it had won from PARC. A year after the Macintosh launch, Microsoft launched Windows, soon to become the undisputed industry standard, underlining the riskiness of Apple's variety-reducing, closed architecture strategy.

But the story isn't over yet: Microsoft's subsequent attempt to reduce variety in operating systems by encouraging PC-makers to standardize on Windows has been called into question recently by the emergence of Linux – a free, or 'open source', operating system, applications for which are being developed by open source aficionados who make them available on the Web free of charge. Microsoft is very worried about Linux and the open source movement. In November 1998, a leaked internal Microsoft document warned that the open source system could muster creative resources that far exceeded those available to a commercial software company.[4]

In brief, the warning embedded in the Law of Requisite Variety is 'don't put all your eggs (or any other protein) in one basket'. The key message to organizations is to ensure that, while they maintain consistency of strategic intent, they also generate variety in structure, product, process, customer and, most importantly, people.

There is a striking lack of diversity within today's organizations. At a recent summit of European business leaders, the ethnicity, educational background, political stance and age of all 170 delegates were almost identical, and almost all were male. In a recent study of a major European automotive manufacturer, A.T. Kearney found that managers in a random sample had on average 20 years' experience in that industry, 19 of which were with their present employer.

With such homogeneity, it is hard to imagine where businesses will find the variety needed to drive innovation.

Multiple interpretations: laminated thinking

What we do with incoming signals is critical. The interpretation, or 'map', we create of our circumstances will govern the agility of our response. As we pointed out in Chapter 1, 'the map is not the territory';[5] in other words, one interpretation of reality can never fully represent that reality. The more maps you have about any given situation, the more choice you have of how to respond. One map or model is fundamentalist; two maps create a dilemma; three or more give freedom of choice.

The British motorcycle industry dominated the world market until the early 1960s, when demand for smaller-capacity machines began to soar and Japanese manufacturers, led by Honda, entered the international market. The response of leading UK firms, such as Triumph, BSA, Norton and Royal Enfield, was to limit the potential for growth and wider variety, by concentrating on larger, higher margin 'superbikes', leaving the smaller-capacity segment to the Japanese. The UK manufacturers' map of the industry simply didn't accommodate the possibility that dominance in the smaller capacity segment would be critical. It was a fatal mistake. The British industry was wiped out when, having stolen the low end of the market, the Japanese manufacturers attacked the high end with better distribution and much greater economies of scale. After several false dawns, the UK industry has recently staged a come-back with a revived Triumph, but the market is still largely owned by the Japanese.

A process called 'chunking' is useful when seeking to increase the diversity of the maps you produce and therefore the options available to you. Chunking varies the focus of your thought framework. 'Chunking up' shifts your thinking to a more general level; for example grouping cars with trains, boats and aeroplanes as 'vehicles'. 'Chunking down' is moving to a more specific level; dismantling 'car', for instance, into tyres, engine, brakes or transmission. You can also chunk 'laterally', by finding similar cases at the same level; 'driving a car' is analogous to 'riding a horse', for example, 'pedalling a bicycle' or 'sailing a boat'.

A lot of business thinking can be understood in terms of chunking. Strategy is chunked down from vision, operations are chunked down from strategy. A decision to diversify is an example of lateral chunking from an existing business. Different levels are appropriate for different situations. High abstract levels will be required in strategy formulation, but lower levels will be required when it comes to testing the practicality of the strategic idea.

Chunking up and down can also open up new avenues for lateral chunking. One could say, for example, that it was Canon's chunking down from 'camera', to optics, electronics and motors that opened up the lateral route to the 'photocopier'. It was a matter of dismantling the camera, and reassembling the components into something else, or to put it another way, to seeing the camera as a metaphor for a general class of products that also included the photocopier.

When the electronics industry began taking off in the late 1950s, following the invention of the transistor, circuit manufacturers were finding it hard to find people with the skills needed to install tiny components on printed circuit boards. The problem seemed insoluble, at one level, because no such devices had been made before. But by chunking down 'circuit assemblers', to 'people with deft fingers and keen eyesight, who could work accurately over long periods', they opened up an avenue for lateral chunking that led them to the armies of needlewomen working as 'invisible menders' for laundry and dry cleaning companies.

Chunking down can tame what Collins and Porras call BHAGs – 'Big Hairy Audacious Goals'[6] – and make apparently overwhelming problems more manageable. Chunking up can transform negative concepts or judgements, such as 'problem' and 'failure', into more positive (and often more appropriate) descriptions, such as 'challenge' and 'feedback'. Chunking laterally, or engaging in what anthropologist Gregory Bateson called metaphorical, or 'abductive' (as distinct from inductive and deductive) thinking,[7] may produce analogies and metaphors containing elegant solutions to apparently insoluble problems, and reveal previously undreamed of opportunities.

There is nothing new about chunking. It is as old as thought itself, and our language is littered with references to it. 'You can't see the wood for the trees'; 'How do you eat an elephant? One bite at a time'; 'From the general to the particular'; 'Bird's-eye view, worm's eye view'; or, as native Americans say, 'Seeing with the eyes of a mouse, or an eagle'. We do it all the time, unconsciously, but an awareness of the process and the ability to move between the levels at will are important components of what we mean by the mental agility required to cross boundaries.

Bounded agility: knowing your part

The paradox of mental agility is the need to operate across boundaries, but within the limits of your core goal or purpose.

Variety is a blessing and a curse – a blessing because, without it, there is no spice to life, and no creativity and agility in a business; a curse because with too much of it, things fall apart and centres cannot hold. The poison is in the dose, and the appropriate dose of variety is enough, but no more than enough, to regulate effectively.

Kevin Kelly makes this point powerfully when he writes 'the Net is a possibility factory . . . [that] will drown the unprepared . . . [in its] debilitating abundance of competing possibilities'.[8]

Leaders must have enough options to regulate all the variety coming at them from their marketplaces, but not so many options that they are spoiled for choice. Too little adaptability can lead to stagnation, rigidity and death, but too much can lead to indecisiveness, and an inability to persevere with a strategy or a course of action long enough to test its worth.

Organizations are what they are, and an important part of the leader's role is to teach his or her organization to know itself. During the electronics revolution PARC behaved as if Xerox was more than a photocopier company; as if its technological, production, marketing and distribution assets imposed no constraints on what it could do and become; as if the whole of the brave new world of microelectronics was its for the taking.

To be creative, mental agility needs to be constrained within themes. Itzhak Perlman's is the violin, Spielberg's is film, Walt Disney's extended beyond film, but was constrained within the theme of 'entertaining children', with animation, conventional film and theme parks.

Lyons Tea Houses were famous in England in the first half of the 20th century, and grew by branding and systematizing tea drinking in a way that is reminiscent of today's branded coffee shops. A by-product of Lyons's success was the need to make ordering and delivery more efficient to deal with increasing complexity and volume. By the early 1950s, the Cadby Hall factory complex which managed the supply chain for the tea houses needed an army of clerks to run it.

As BBC journalist Mark Whittaker reports: 'The company that believed it could do anything decided to build a business computer, and did so with considerable success.' Lyons called their computer Leo, and it ran the world's first real business program. Leo was so successful that Lyons did work for other companies and for the British government: for example, calculating new tax tables on the night of the Chancellor's budget, and working out the distance between every one of British Rail's 5000 stations.

Lyons promoted this early computer and managed to sell 80 of them. However, it soon became clear that the early buyers in the computer market were much happier buying from a company called International Business Machines than they were from Lyons Tea House. The Leo venture died in the 1960s, beaten by 'the perception that a catering company couldn't build computers'.[9]

A successful business leader's mental agility is constrained within a clear vision of where the organization is equipped to go, and what its 'essence' (whether expressed in terms of its 'core competencies', its customers or its meta-brand or personality) allows it to become.

But it should be no ordinary vision. When Disney was interviewed soon after the opening of his animated classic *Fantasia*, he was asked what he expected the future to be like. His reply was typically short on detail, and long on grandeur. 'The future is big,' he said, 'and it glitters.'[10] Goals and visions liberate, as well as constrain, and the more variations they have, the more liberating they become. As Friedrich Nietzsche said: 'It is good to express a matter in two ways simultaneously, so as to give it both a right foot and a left. Truth can stand on one leg to be sure; but with two it can walk and get about.'[11]

Canon's essence in the late 1970s could have been expressed as 'We're good at making cameras', which might have constrained its development to similar product areas such as cine and slide projectors and later to video cameras. But its essence could and effectively was also expressed as 'We know about optics, electronics and electric motors'. Both expressions of the company's essence were true, but adding the second allowed it to 'get about' and walk into the photocopier market.

When wrestling with the paradox inherent in the concept of bounded agility, keep the mantra of 'fixed goals, variable means' in mind. Hold fast to your goal, but be ready to adapt your route to that goal. One business school professor of strategy bases his strategic planning with clients on a big picture vision of success, coupled with a highly flexible means of getting there. He and his clients identify the five best things about the company and design projects to enhance them, and identify the five worst things about the company and design projects to reduce them. Liberated from the need to predict a precise route to future success, the company can focus on what it does best and how to use that ability to achieve its core goal.

Flexibility in the face of obstacles: there is no failure, only feedback

Scientists and inventors have always 'chunked up' failures to feedback. For them, failure is the essential foundation of subsequent success, because it eliminates dead ends, opens up new routes and piques their curiosity. Isaac Asimov once said: 'The most exciting phrase to hear in science, the one that heralds new discoveries, is not "eureka!!", but "that's funny . . .".'[12] Curiosity is another essential component of mental agility, and it feeds on failure, but only where failure is viewed as an opportunity to learn more, to explore new avenues, rather than as a signal to give up or, worse, to apportion blame.

When 31-year-old Thomas Edison announced his intention, in 1878, to perfect the incandescent light bulb, invented in 1860 by the English physicist, Sir Joseph Swan, gas stocks tumbled in New York and London. Edison had already improved the telephone and invented the stock ticker and the phonograph. Stock markets had little doubt that, with the 'Wizard of Menlo Park' on the case, the days of the gas lamp were numbered.

Edison was confident too because he had great faith in his trial and error method, but it was not the easiest of his inventive triumphs. His goal was clear enough: he needed a wire that could be heated to incandescence by an electric current within an evacuated glass chamber, but he found it hard to find a metal that would stand the intense heat for long periods. He spent a year and $50 000 on proving that platinum wire was no good.

After thousands of experiments, Edison found, as Swan had discovered nearly 20 years earlier, that the answer was carbon in the form of scorched cotton thread, or (in Swan's case) strips of carbonized paper. Swan had struggled for years to create a good vacuum, and only solved the problem in 1879, the year Edison demonstrated his bulb and secured patent 222 898.

The roads to the incandescent light bulb were littered on both sides of the Atlantic with broken glass and melted metal; the detritus of many thousands of failed experiments. Inventors test their ideas to destruction and, each time, find new inspiration in the wreckage. The longer success eludes them, the more curious and determined they become. Before Chester Carlson finally perfected a practical 'xerography' (from the Greek 'dry writing') copier in 1960, he built devices he knew wouldn't work, because he needed to know why they wouldn't work. Test pilots adopt a similar strategy. Each time they go up, they push the new aeroplane a little further, because they know that the plane will only reveal its fragilities when it starts to break up.

Lowell Noble of QD Technology, a 3D imaging company in Silicon Valley, ran approximately 50 000 experiments before finally developing a winning technology. In his description of this process lies the key to the state of mind essential to this form of mental agility: 'I guess I didn't consider them failures. I just figured they were solutions to a problem other than the one I was working on at the time.'

Tools for thought

1. Securing variety

How well do you and your organization meet the challenges of Requisite Variety? Ask yourself the following questions:

- How alike are you? Is there a high degree of commonality among the people who work for your organization? How many years has management been in the same industry/company? How can you build more diversity into your employee and management pool?
- Who are the outsiders? What are they saying? How does this differ from accepted wisdom? If they are right, what implications does this have for the future of your organization?
- Is variety being overregulated? Are there too many chiefs, and too many rules? Is there only one 'right' way of doing things? If so, how can you reduce, 'relax' or redistribute rule making?
- Is the organization overspecialized, or too wedded to services or products that have been successful in the past? What percentage of revenue comes from new products or services? This year? Last year? Are all your eggs in one basket? If so, what other options or choices can you add to your repertoire of activities or portfolio of products and services?
- How alike are your customers? Who do you listen to? When you conduct market research, what do you do with the outlying responses? Ignore or question? If the outliers pointed to a possible future trend, what implications would this have for your products and marketing strategy?
- Does your 'system' feel overloaded? Is there insufficient control to absorb the variety affecting you? If so, what can be done to reduce

variety? What skills, capabilities or tools could you add that would make it easier to achieve your goals?

• Does the organization seem powerless or dependent? Does it rely too much on others to regulate variety? If so, what other ways are open to you, to get what you need?

2. Clarity of goals and purpose: chunking up and down

Chunking can be useful in gaining clarity regarding your goal, or in exploring possible obstacles to the achievement of that goal in a way that readily translates into a pragmatic plan of action.

In a Californian study in the 1950s, students were asked if they had written personal goals – only 3% did. Twenty-five years later, the students were surveyed again. The 3% with written goals were worth more than the other 97% put together.

You cannot succeed without a goal to measure success, but it is sometimes hard to decide what your goal should be. 'Chunking up' can help you solve this problem. It can turn a prosaic, uninspiring objective into a compelling goal or purpose that you and others will be motivated to achieve together.

Start by identifying what you want to achieve, for example, a successful product launch or a more flexible way of behaving with a difficult colleague. Ask yourself, or your team, if we achieved this goal, what would it do for us? Apply the question again to the answer you get. (See Figure 2.1.)

Chunking up might translate into 'a successful product launch would help penetrate the Asian market'. Ask yourself again, 'If we got this, what would this do for us?' Answer: 'Our brand would become known in the Asian market', and so on. Figure 2.2 demonstrates this hierarchy of goals and continues the chunking-up process.

Keep going until you reach a high enough goal to make sense without becoming too general (stop before you get to achieving world peace!). Look again at the top of your pyramid of outcomes. What does this tell you about your mission? What does it say about how to restate your objectives in a way that will engage more with the energy of your team?

You are more likely to achieve a goal if you break the goal down into its component parts. The simplest way of chunking down is to ask yourself the question: 'What do I need to do to achieve this?'

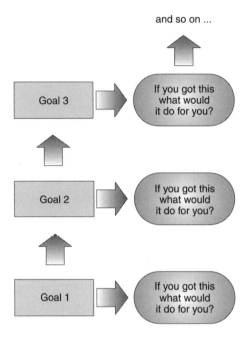

Figure 2.1 *Chunking up*

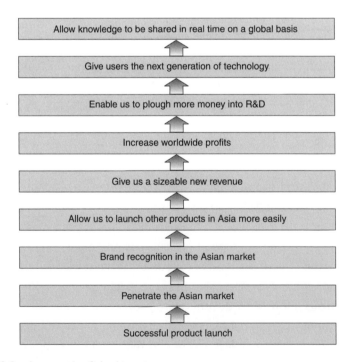

Figure 2.2 *An example of chunking up*

This process can be repeated on each of your answers to give you a detailed project plan. For example, if your goal is 'Persuade the boss to give me a pay rise', then you might have several subgoals as illustrated in Figure 2.3.

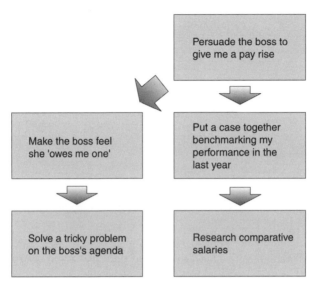

Figure 2.3 *Simple chunking down*

To tackle more difficult problems, a more sophisticated chunking-down process can be used which focuses on roadblocks and barriers to success. Start with a specific outcome you want to achieve. What stops you achieving it? Continue asking this question until you have identified all potential limitations as shown in Figure 2.4. For each limitation then ask, what do you want instead? Keep going, asking for each of these outcomes, what stops you achieving them, and what do you want instead, until you feel comfortable that all potential barriers have been identified. Use the limitations and outcomes you have identified to create an effective and pragmatic action plan.

For example, Joe wanted to change the atmosphere in his management team, and create a 'no blame culture'. His goal was to create a culture of collective responsibility in his team. He asked himself 'What stops us from achieving that?' and came up with the answer: 'Senior management likes someone to shoot when things go wrong.'

Continuing the process, he came up with the following questions and answers:

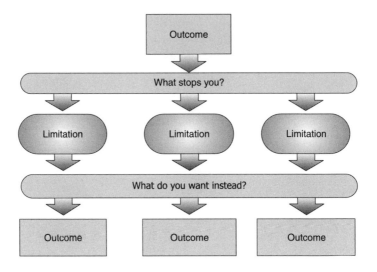

Figure 2.4 *Chunking down: identifying obstacles*

Q. What do I want instead?

A. Refusal by the team to be divided and to allow scape-goating, that is to say, the team standing together.

Q. What stops us from achieving that?

A. Lack of trust between team members. Instead I want trust.

Q. What *else* prevents the team from standing together?

A. Insufficient benefits in working together.

Q. What do I want instead?

A. People to be aware of what we can create if we mutually support each other, and an understanding of the impact on all of our careers.

And so on, down to the fundamental next steps as described in Figure 2.5.

3. Varying means

The practical value of Ashby's Law of Requisite Variety lies in the way it can help us to increase our mental and behavioural flexibility in response to new, difficult or complex situations.

Ashby's law says that, 'the element in the system which has the most flexibility is the element that controls the system'. A translation into the human realm might be that the person with the most choice in his or her behaviour is the person most able to influence the course of future events.

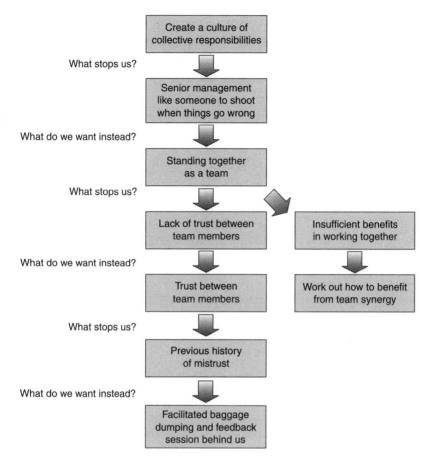

Figure 2.5 *Example of chunking down*

The more variety you have in your behaviour, the more chance you will develop a strategy or a tactic that will achieve the desired result. Most of the time we do this instinctively, but once we have tried a number of different options, it is easy to become disillusioned and give up, or to modify our goal. It is here that the mentally agile leader's special qualities kick in. To start with, keep your goal stable. Leave it alone. Focus on the means.

If the goal you are trying to achieve is a goal in which you want to influence people by the effect of your own behaviour, a key variable will be the extent to which you have personal flexibility in your own style. The more personal flexibility you have, the broader the range of behaviours open to you, the more easily you will find a way to achieve your objective. You may need to be very humble or very assertive; very sensitive or very macho; do a

46468

lot of listening or do a lot of talking; 'play dead' or be very much alive; be the consummate politician or the silent action hero or heroine.

Our behavioural flexibility is limited. When we reach those limits, one more strategy is left to adapt the means to your goal. Take the goal, and ask yourself: 'What would be another way to achieve this goal?' Keep asking the question, and try some wild answers to stimulate your thinking.

Try again by asking a slightly different question, 'What is the purpose of this goal?', and then: 'What would be another way of achieving that purpose?' to see if this elicits any more variation.

In this way you can ensure maximum flexibility in the achievement of your overall purpose. Perhaps the slogan 'fixed goals, variable means' would be more appropriately expressed as 'fixed purpose, responsive goals, variable means'.

The following case is an example of applying the principles of chunking up and down, and 'fixed purpose, responsive goals, variable means' to an on-going operational problem.

James was a manufacturing director who wanted to influence the CEO to implement a new manufacturing system. The old overhead system for moving engines through the assembly process was antiquated, and engines had to be manually lifted on and off the system at various workstations so that they could be rotated. A modern 'smart' system would allow the engines to be lowered, raised and rotated, as well as enabling the managers to control the work rate by varying the speed of the system and the transport of engines between workstations. Combined with other new plant, state of the art manufacturing philosophy and right-first-time manufacturing methods, the engines could be produced to a higher quality, with less rework, and lower labour costs.

James used the chunking-down tools described above. He created a cost–benefit analysis, persuaded three other directors to champion the proposal, dealt with some blockers and even put together a marketing case based on the impact of the new systems on dealers who visited the factory. However, the industry was in recession and the CEO would not authorize the expenditure, even though he agreed with the proposals in principle.

Rather than resign himself to a suboptimized assembly hall, James got creative and chunked sideways to another goal. 'What would a new manufacturing system achieve?' Answer: 'A more efficient manufacturing system.' 'What would be another way of achieving that?' Answer: 'Focus on key improvement areas.' 'What is stopping us from focusing on key improvement areas?' Answer: 'No energy in the Total Quality programme, so what we want instead is to reenergize the TQ programme.' 'What else can we do to improve our manufacturing?'

Answer: 'Introduce right-first-time manufacturing philosophy and manufacturing process control.'

James kept chunking his goal through 'A more efficient manufacturing system' to 'More durable fault-free engines', right up to 'More customer satisfaction'. He then asked himself, 'What would be another way of achieving more customer satisfaction?' His answer was, 'Improve the speed of warranty service'. When new cars go wrong, cars should be away from the owner for the shortest amount of time and with the minimum of inconvenience. Even though James could not implement a new manufacturing system, he could increase customer satisfaction by improving warranty service, and he could reduce the likelihood of faults in the engines by improvement strategies that included a revitalized total quality programme and other manufacturing improvements (Figure 2.6).

Figure 2.6 *James' solution*

For more resources on developing mental agility, visit www.AlphaLeaders.com

Conclusion

Mental agility is critical. Without it, organizations will not benefit from the early detection of weak signals in the market. Agile leaders know how to innovate across boundaries, while also holding steadfastly to their core purpose – they 'know their part', but are not hidebound in the way they deliver it.

Organizational diversity is a key component in building the mental agility of leaders. The ability to build multiple interpretations, or 'maps', of any given circumstance will strongly influence the organization's responsiveness.

In Chapter 3, we will explore the resource fluidity that is necessary to translate a leader's mental agility into effective action.

References

1. Riemer, J. (1995) Itzhak Perlman improvises, *Houston Chronicle*, November.
2. Bateson, G. (1972) *Steps to an Ecology of Mind*, Ballantine Books.
3. Ashby, W. (1957) *An Introduction to Cybernetics*, Wiley.
4. Taylor, R. (1998) USA: 'Anarchists' take on the big boys, *Financial Times*, 7 December.
5. Korzybski, A. (1980) *Science and Sanity*, the International Non-Aristotelian Library, Lakeville, CN.
6. Collins, J. and Porras, J. (1994) *Built to Last: Successful Habits of Visionary Companies*, Harper Business.
7. Bateson (1972) *Op. cit.*
8. Kelly, K. (1997) New rules for the New Economy: Twelve dependable principles for thriving in a turbulent world, *Wired*, September.
9. Whittaker, M. (presenter) (2001) *Electronic Brains: Leo the Lyons Computer*, BBC Radio 4, October 30 (Pennine Radio production for BBC).
10. *Growing Pains*, by Walt Disney, originally quoted in *Journal of SMPE*, 1941; reprinted in *Journal of SMPTE*, July 1991.
11. Attributed to Friedrich Nietzsche, http://www.stats.gla.ac.uk/wernst/redundan.html.
12. Attributed to Isaac Asimov, http://www.brainyquote.com/quotes/quotes/i/q109758.html.

3

Freeing-up Resources

Freedom is chaos, with better lighting
Alan Dean Foster

In early June 1942, US naval reconnaissance planes spotted a huge Japanese fleet of 185 ships, including nine battleships and four aircraft carriers, heading for the Midway Islands in the central Pacific. Under the command of Admiral Yamamoto Isoroku, commander-in-chief of the Japanese navy and chief architect of the attack on Pearl Harbor, the armada's apparent mission was to secure the islands as a launch pad for an invasion of Hawaii.

On the morning of 4 June, planes from the Japanese carriers attacked airfields on Midway, and American planes from Midway and three US aircraft carriers of the Pacific Fleet, under the command of Admiral Chester W. Nimitz, attacked the Japanese fleet. The Japanese attacks inflicted damage on the Midway airbases, but failed to prevent American planes from refuelling and rejoining the battle. The American dive-bombers were much more incisive. In one five-minute attack they destroyed three Japanese carriers. They sank the fourth later that day.

The American victory at Midway was the turning point in the Pacific War. It was a victory against the odds, because, with only 10 ships (three carriers and seven heavy cruisers), and the aircraft from Midway, the Americans destroyed all four of Yamamoto's aircraft carriers, two cruisers and three destroyers, for the loss of the carrier *Yorktown* and one destroyer. And it was a very unusual naval engagement in that during the two-day battle, the two fleets never got close enough to exchange gunfire, let alone to see one another.

Radio also played an interesting role in the battle. The advantage of surprise, which Yamamoto was right to expect would be crucial, but wrong to expect would be his, went to the Americans. Nimitz, an avid 'weak signal' eavesdropper, was monitoring Japanese radio messages and, as a result, had early warning of the impending attack and was able to prepare for battle.

In addition, radio was used to better effect by the Americans than the Japanese during the battle itself. The remoteness of the two commanders from their airborne strike forces made it very hard for them to orchestrate their forces directly. The omnipotence of the commander in the Japanese military tradition obliged Yamamoto to try to do so, but the pace at which air battles are fought meant that his radio instructions simply confused his pilots. Nimitz and Rear Admiral Raymond A. Spruance, commander of the US carrier task force, made no attempt to direct the battle, but instead established simple rules of communication: keep all radio channels to other planes open; listen, but say nothing unless you are coming under attack from enemy fighters or you are in a position to attack an enemy ship.

These rules were decisive because they generated powerful, self-organizing dynamics among the American planes that caused them to gather rapidly in critical areas of airspace. Although heavily outnumbered, the US pilots flew in overwhelming force to where they were most needed.

In one sense, the Battle of Midway was won before it began; not through the assembly of superior force, or by a brilliant battlefield commander, but by sensitivity to weak signals, the commander's recognition of the limitations of command in a fast-moving situation, the care Nimitz took in choosing his subordinates and the freedom he gave them to use their initiative.

One of the key themes of this book is that 'leadership' is not really about individuals at all, but about the relationship between leaders and the led. Leaders who can detect weak signals, can read the threats and opportunities they presage and have the mental agility to devise appropriate responses to them will remain powerless if their organizations lack the flexibility to redirect their energies and reassign their resources quickly. In the end, it is not what the leader does that matters, but what the led do, how quickly they do it and how easy it is for them to get hold of the resources they need to do it right.

In this chapter we will look at how a leader can create an organization that has a high degree of self-organization and adaptability; with lean structures to handle the day-to-day, monthly and annual repetitive tasks, and a pool of highly talented people able to 'swarm' around special projects that will drive the business forward. This organization is lean *and* it has the flexibility to respond to weak signals at short notice; it is minimalist *and* has time to think and be creative. The more self-organizing the business, the more the leader can focus on the special tasks of leadership (see Chapter 7: 80:20 Leadership).

The story of the Battle of Midway provides us with a powerful lesson on how to create adaptive and flexible organizations, able to put their ability to detect weak signals and their leaders' mental agility to practical use. It highlights three vital qualities of adaptable organizations: they operate by simple rules, their resources are free to move, and they understand the value of redundancy. These are the qualities that drive the self-organizing power of what complexity theorists call 'complex adaptive systems'.

Rules, not commands

Nature is alive with self-organization generated by a few simple rules. The flocking behaviour of birds, for instance, seems very complex, but it can be reproduced on a computer with just three rules, identified by Craig Reynolds in his research on coordinated animal movement called 'Boids':[1]

- Rule 1. Separation (steer to avoid crowding local flockmates).
- Rule 2. Alignment (steer towards the average heading of local flockmates).
- Rule 3. Cohesion (steer to move towards the average position of local flockmates).

It is worth watching Reynolds' program of 'boids' flocking that you can access at his Website at http://www.red3d.com/cwr/boids/applet/. Each 'boid' is designed as an autonomous unit, but each is guided by a common set of rules. When the flock meets a new obstacle, each 'boid' individually 'makes its mind up' about how to apply the rules to its current circumstances, and as a result the whole flock successfully navigates its way around the obstacle.

Equally, the apparently 'organized' behaviour of ant colonies is not the result of top-down instructions – it emerges from the rule-governed interactions between individuals. Although the rules are simple, such as 'Follow the pheromone trails left by other ants', when all ants obey them, the colony as a whole can solve difficult problems, such as finding the shortest route among an enormous number of possible routes to a food source.

The famous 'travelling salesman problem' appeals to mathematicians because it is easy to state ('Find the shortest route that visits a given number of cities once'), but impossible to solve, because the number of computational steps required to solve it grows faster than the number of cities. For only 15 cities, for example, there are billions of possible routes. The only way to tackle such problems is to abandon hope of finding the best solution and settle instead for a 'good enough' solution. Scientists have recently shown that ant-based systems, in which software 'ants' lay and follow the equivalent of pheromone trails, are extremely good at finding near-optimal solutions to the travelling salesman type of problem.

So-called 'swarm intelligence' is being applied to a wide range of business areas. Ant-based algorithms have been used to find the best locations for, and routes between, the storage tanks, mixing machines and packing lines in factories. France Telecom, BT and MCI Worldcom are interested in using them to reroute traffic in their networks. Task allocation in honeybee colonies has led to a new approach to scheduling paint booths in a truck factory, and the way social insects sort their larvae and their dead has led to new ways of analysing banking data.[2]

Several consulting boutiques, such as BiosGroup, i2 Technologies and Artificial Life, have recently been set up to apply complexity principles to business, and have received backing from mainstream consulting firms and large companies, such as Ford Motor Company and Procter & Gamble. Companies are beginning to realize that establishing a few simple rules is the first step to achieving effective resource mobility and distributed decision making. You as leaders need to find the simple rules that can create a framework within which your companies can self-organize effectively.

Leadership is a resource, and it is a misuse of the leadership resource to use it on micromanagement and operational details, when establishing a few simple rules will liberate the organization's self-organizing power. There is an enormous amount employees will do very well without being told — much more than most leaders realize. We are not talking here about 'empowerment' (the 'you are empowered to do anything, so long as it is what I wanted you to do' fad of the 1990s), but about the inherent ability of complex adaptive systems to find elegant solutions to difficult problems by following simple rules.

Structures that can flex

Simple rules will only lead to effective self-organization if the structure of the organization is flexible. Simple rules need open space. If they have to operate within a rigid framework, they cannot generate self-organization, because people and assets cannot move to the point of greatest impact. Many consultancy firms learned this the hard way when they organized by country, region and specialism. When people are imprisoned in a rigid matrix, cross-boundary business development and project staffing is rare, and the service to clients suffers accordingly.

When organizational boundaries are made more permeable, results improve. A.T. Kearney has three profit centres (Europe, the Americas and Asia). Staff are encouraged to cross geographical boundaries, and 'functional' teams are affiliations dedicated to promoting learning and the cross-fertilization of ideas, rather than profit categories that dictate staffing decisions. This fluid structure has helped Kearney grow faster than its competitors and, at the same time, to deliver superior customer service.[3]

Freedom of movement at every level reduces the 'control' of the leader, but increases the agility and creativity of the organization. The answer is not to throw out structures entirely, but to select those that best mirror the needs of the market and maximize the flexibility of response. The staff of corporate communications departments, for instance, used to specialize in particular kinds of media, such as external print and broadcast or internal newsletter. The best practice emerging in corporate communications is to organize around projects or events. This is better for the constituencies being communicated with, because it is the event, such as a product launch or factory fire, that matters, rather than the type of media it is reported in. It is better from the organization's point of view, too, because most events are reported in several media and the organization's response to them needs to be swift, authoritative and consistent.

The location of decision making can also affect the extent to which a complex system can organize itself. Air traffic control, a system near collapse due to the massive growth in air travel, illustrates the point.

At present, each air traffic controller manages one segment of airspace, and 'holds the picture' by updating blips on his or her screen with data from communications, navigation and surveillance (CNS) systems on speed, courses and rates of descent or climb.

The only way to increase the capacity of such a system is to divide the air corridors into ever smaller segments. Because controllers can only handle a limited number of aircraft at once, however, and spend most of their time managing handovers into and out of their sectors, this strategy is subject to diminishing returns and is now close to its limits on busy routes (hence the increase in delays and 'stacking').

The answer is to let computers 'hold the picture', and have the controllers and pilots manage by exception. Computers can process data far more quickly than conscious human minds, and can therefore reduce the separation between aircraft deemed to be 'safe' far closer to the physical limits imposed by a plane's wake and inertia.

But where should the computers be: on the ground in a centralized system or airborne in a distributed system known as 'free flight', where aircraft get CNS feeds, communicate with each other and organize their own separation? A centralized system is simply a computerized version of the existing system, and may therefore prove more politically acceptable. But 'free flight' (an adaptation of the Midway system in that aircraft say 'I'm here, keep your distance', rather than 'I've found a target, or I am under attack, come and help') would be cheaper and more flexible.

Of course, not all companies are able to flex their structures as easily as project-based organizations, such as consultancies or communications departments. No one would want on-going processes like finance or manufacturing to be run as one-off projects.

However, significant change is so common that many staff now spend their working lives moving from project to project. This may be unsettling, but it is the future. Our job security lies in our competencies, not our organizational position. In Chapter 5 (Task Through Relationship) and Chapter 6 (Creating Cultures That Can Act), we will offer some methods for sustaining people's sense of security while allowing them to 'swarm' around organizational hot-spots.

Our research indicates that successful companies will turn increasingly to what Seiriol James, managing director of SGi, calls 'Project World' – a world in which businesses parcel as much of their activities as possible into discrete projects, and in which project management skills reign supreme.

James asserts that 'organizations which do not adopt a Project World approach to business and change will continue to fail to deliver to timescale, to budget, and to specification, and will encounter a costly impact to their competitiveness in the market'.[4] He contrasts Project World with the business-as-usual culture, in which the focus is on repetitive, hierarchical and departmental processes within a single management structure. The management of projects requires a focus on outcomes rather than activities, on short-term and transient teams, on delivery promises, and spans several management layers and organizational boundaries – characteristics that have a lot in common with the day-to-day activities of today's networked and results-oriented organizations.

Indeed in manufacturing, repetitive processes are increasingly outsourced to contract manufacturers, who do see manufacturing as a series of limited range contracts or projects. Even the car industry, inventor of the production line, views manufacturing as a series of multiyear product programmes. In this context, we believe that traditional organizations can learn to benefit from the resource and structural fluidity enjoyed by project-based companies.

Resource mobility in practice: the Oticon story

The success of Danish hearing-aid company, Oticon, illustrates the power of simple rules and fluid structures in business.

When Lars Kolind was appointed CEO in 1988, Oticon was losing money. Kolind responded conventionally by cutting costs and increasing productivity. After the company was back in the black, however, he realized that more had to be done if Oticon was not to be overwhelmed by the likes of Sony, Siemens and Philips.

On New Year's Day 1990, Kolind issued a memo to staff, saying Oticon needed break-through products, that such products would require a 'combination of technology with audiology, psychology and imagination', and staff had 'to think the unthinkable and make it happen'. He said that in organizations of the future, 'staff would be liberated to grow personally and professionally and . . . become more creative, action-oriented and efficient'. He argued that the enemy of such organizations was organization itself so he abolished the formal organization. Projects, not functions or processes, are the units of work. Teams form, disband and reform. Project leaders (anyone with an idea) compete for resources and people. Project owners (members of the management team) provide advice and support, but make few decisions.

The most significant of several subsequent break-throughs came in 1995 with the launch of 'DigiFocus', the world's first ear-level digital hearing aid.

Oticon employees have no titles or offices, and paper is anathema. 'We give people the freedom to do what they want,' Kolind told *Fast Company*. 'We are developing products twice as fast as anyone else . . . [but in] a very relaxed atmosphere. We're not fast on the surface; we're fast underneath.' When one project got so big it became 'organized', Kolind broke it up, in a rare top management intervention. 'It was total chaos,' he recalled proudly. 'Within three hours over 100 people had moved.' He thinks that one of the main jobs of management is to 'keep the company disorganized'.[5]

When Kolind resigned as President in May 1998, he left the company in excellent health. The hearing aid market was static in the 1990s, but Oticon's sales and profits rose strongly and in October 2000, *Forbes Global* ranked its parent company, William Demant Holding (WDH), among the world's 20 best small companies. The criteria for this honour are that the company should be publicly quoted, have annual sales of less than $500 million, have recorded good earnings growth over the previous three years and be expected by stock analysts to continue to do so in the current year. The WDH shares had quadrupled in price over the previous 12 months, and the profits of the company (of which Oticon is the only asset) had grown by 25% in each of the previous eight years.

Kolind was not a conventional leader. He issued few commands apart from the exhortation to 'think the unthinkable' and formulated no strategies, unless his declaration that 'we need break-throughs' can be construed as such. The simple rules were that there are no rules, and that people should 'flock' to the projects that seem most promising or they find most interesting, just as American warplanes 'flocked' during the Battle of Midway. The temptation is to try to reduce uncertainty and variety. Kolind showed that, if you try to *absorb*, rather than reduce them, you will stimulate innovation. Oticon's digital hearing aid is very simple, but as Kolind understood, simplicity is an emergent quality, and creation itself is an inherently complex and messy process.

Replacing commands with simple rules, and substituting fluid, market facing units for rigid structures, gives an organization the counterpart of the mental agility of its leader. By allowing resources to move, without being told, to where they are most needed, leaders can get away from the details and do some serious thinking. They will still be available in emergencies, but 'leading by exception' will improve their anticipatory powers by giving them more time to attend to and ponder the implications of weak signals. Be warned, however. When you adopt this approach to making your resources more agile, you will be confronted by a paradox.

Good redundancy?

Although self-organization and freedom to 'flock' leads to a more efficient use of resources, it requires a certain amount of redundancy. There will be no flocking if people are exclusively focused on their own areas. Corridor and water-cooler conversations are the essential fuel of self-organization. The staircase in Oticon's headquarters was deliberately built wider than it needed to be to accommodate up-and-down traffic, so that people had room to stop and chat.

As we shall see in Chapter 7, well-led organizations 'stretch' resources in the same way that, as we saw in Chapter 2, Perlman 'stretched' three strings to do the work of four. But, because it is impossible to know beforehand what will be needed when an issue arises, they also keep resources in reserve. Such contingency reserves may seem 'redundant' to a leader who looks at everything to ensure that it is contributing to the overall goal, but they are not redundant in the same way as the parasites or passengers, in the form of superfluous processes or people, that organizations pick up over time and then fail to dispense with when they have outlived their usefulness. An actor who understudies a star is not wasting her time, she is preparing to take the place of the star if the need arises.

As Kevin Kelly has pointed out: 'wasting time and being inefficient are the way to discovery . . . While 40 year old boomers can't take a vacation without thinking how they'll justify the trip as being productive, the young can follow hunches and create seemingly mindless novelties . . . without wondering whether they are being efficient. Out of these inefficient tinkerings will come the future.'[6]

When you have to be alert for weak signals and handle ambiguity, you need to keep some resources in reserve that may sometimes be wasted, simply because they may sometimes prove essential.

The 'corporate anorexia' (cutting resources to the bone) many organizations have fallen victim to carries hidden costs: revenue loss, because you don't have time to nurture the customer, missed market share through insufficient reflection on emergent trends and opportunities, and, perhaps most damaging of all, the loss of key staff who decide to move on rather than wait to see where the axe will fall next. In the minutes of a board meeting of a global services firm, there was a plaintive, one-line item at the end of pages of discussion on cost-cutting initiatives, which tasked a director to 'improve staff morale' in order to address high staff turnover!

So how can you distinguish between reserves that are the price you must pay for mobility, and reserves that are a complete waste? Research on imitation and learning provides some clues.

Monkey see, monkey do

Experiments with human children and young chimpanzees have shown that human children imitate more precisely, but less selectively, than chimps. Chimps imitate large chunks of behaviour, and seem more interested in immediate outcomes than in the imitation process itself. Children imitate everything, mistakes and all. Researchers suggest that the reason why young humans 'ape' procedures more faithfully than apes is that faithful imitation disseminates improvements more quickly through a group. There is simply too much variation in outcome-oriented chimp imitation for small improvements to be noticeable.

In other words, you need redundancy, in the form of more faithful imitation than is required to produce the desired outcome, to spot small improvements.

This same sort of apparent cognitive redundancy may help explain the genius of 'autistic savants', people with severe mental disorders who exhibit extraordinary talents in the field of art, music or mathematics.

One such autistic savant is the artist, Stephen Wiltshire. It seems that he cannot help seeing and remembering every detail of his environment. In one striking demonstration of this faculty, he was taken in a helicopter over London, and asked to draw what he had seen. Over a period of a few hours an extraordinary canvas depicting every last detail of building, bridge, river and street emerged. Wiltshire had, in a short flight, captured every detail of an immensely complex city. His fellow passengers were left with only the vaguest impressions, because their sensory systems had assumed the bulk of detail available to them was 'redundant'. It appears that Wiltshire's ability to turn vast amounts of data into a minutely detailed work of art overloads his cognitive system and impairs other mental functions.

Professor Robyn Young of Flinders University, Southern Australia, has shown that autistic savant abilities can be replicated in healthy volunteers by 'switching off' certain parts of their brains. When strong magnetic pulses disabled their language and social skills temporarily to mimic the symptoms of autism, some of the volunteers were capable of savant abilities, such as superior recall, musical or artistic ability. It seems that other cognitive process, such as using language, prevent us from accessing higher level skills, such as perfect pitch. When we switch off parts of the brain, those apparently 'redundant' skills become accessible.

The difficulty for organizations is that it is impossible to know the worth of any resource until after it is proven. As leaders, we have to place bets without certainty. We know that, to achieve a level of redundancy that will create a masterpiece, we risk overloading the system to such an extent that we cannot operate in other areas. But we also know that if we don't 'switch off' some areas, we will never discover the full potential latent in the organization.

The extraordinary ability Perlman demonstrated to make three violin strings do the work of four was 'redundant' every time he played with four strings, but it came in very handy on 18 November 1995, at the Lincoln Center in New York City.

Real options

The ability to move resources more quickly than your rivals to higher value uses has always been a competitive advantage. Now that intangible assets have replaced tangible assets as the prime movers of business, the ability to free up resources has become even more valuable. Unlike steel mills, chemical plants and factories which are built for 'specific purposes' and can be valued by conventional discounted cash flow (DCF) calculations, intangible assets are 'general purpose' and cannot be valued fully by discounting net cash flows from the uses to which they are currently put.

Steel mills cannot be switched to aluminium smelting, in response to a shift in demand, but knowledge, creativity, brand image, reputation and customer loyalty can be shifted relatively easily between assignments. A steel mill has only one kind of value – the net present value (NPV) of the only use to which it can be put. Knowledge has two kinds of value – the NPV of the uses to which it is being put, and the value of the options to put it to a different use, if and when an opportunity to deploy it more profitably arises.

In recent years, the growing importance of general purpose intangible assets has led to an interest in so-called 'real options' – business options that can be valued by new variants of the pricing models used to value financial options.

Real option advocates argue that in a turbulent business environment, when new opportunities are constantly arising and old plans must be revised or abandoned, conventional accept/reject investment decisions must be replaced by option pricing and 'dynamic' strategic planning. Leaders must always be on the lookout for opportunities to exercise the built-in options of their investment projects. Your strategic plans must evolve, and your investment mix and targets must be periodically revised as you actively try to benefit from new business opportunities or to modify old ones.

Your current growth and return on assets targets, for example, must reflect your latest understanding of your firm's value-maximizing strategy. Leaders can use option-based valuations to draft exercise policies and guidelines, such as 'increase production in year x when the output price exceeds £y, or abandon production when value drops below £z'.

If real options catch on, and ultimately replace DCF analysis in areas such as strategy-formulation and investment appraisal, management and leadership will change radically. Company leaders will need to convince the market, not only that the current deployment of their assets is the most profitable deployment, but also that they and their organizations are willing and able to redeploy their assets very quickly if a more profitable deployment becomes available. This doesn't mean that leaders should chop and change at the heart of their strategy. Constancy of purpose is key, but it is also critical to maximize flexibility in the way assets are deployed to achieve that purpose.

Options are worthless if they are not exercised. Organizations that lack the necessary flexibility to redeploy assets quickly, and whose leaders are not always on the lookout for more profitable deployments of those assets will be vanquished by more agile organizations led by more alert executives.

Tools for thought

1. Minimum rules

All organizations operate under systems of rules. The problem is that the rules are often hidden, that is, they are implicit in the way the organization operates, rather than explicit in its operating procedures and manuals. In order to identify the simple rules you need to self-organize, you will need to reveal these unspoken rules. Some will be helpful or useful; others will be constraining and will need to be addressed.

For example, when working with one professional services firm, it became clear that, although deploying a global team was critical to the delivery of superior customer service, staffing practices dictated that teams were usually made up solely of local professionals. It was necessary to recognize the 'rule' that drove this behaviour: 'Look after the local team first – only deploy international professionals if there is no local team member free, regardless of expertise.' This rule, never written, never expressed, and in direct contravention of the 'official' staffing policy, nevertheless was the strongest driver of staffing practices firmwide. In order to overcome this practice, a series of steps were taken, including the appointment of regional rather than local staffers, and changes to the financial reporting system to overcome the negative impact on local income of staffing international professionals.

One of the quickest ways to uncover hidden rules and to identify the few simple rules you need to allow your business or team to self-organize is to use what Joel Barker, eminent futurist, and his colleague Wayne Bukan, have termed 'accelerator phrases'. The following exercise is adapted from their work on paradigms.[7]

Invite your team to brainstorm descriptions of their situation using the following phrases as a starting point for those descriptions:

- 'It is effective for us to . . .'
- 'We act as if . . .'

The first phrase will surface what is needed to do business effectively. The second will typically surface those practices that impede performance. Capture all inputs on two flip charts. Encourage the group to shout out as many phrases as possible – you will usually find that, given permission, they will have a lot of fun with the second phrase!

Take the phrases starting 'It is effective for us to . . .'. Synthesize the phrases into clusters and try to distill each cluster of phrases into one simple rule. For example, phrases such as 'It is effective for us to . . . work with colleagues from other offices . . . team internationally . . . draw on colleagues with the best expertise wherever they come from . . . cross borders' can be translated into the rule 'always team internationally'. Keep going until you have distilled all the ideas into a few simple rules.

Take the phrases starting 'We act as if . . .'. Do the same exercise of synthesis and distillation until you have summarized the group's input. Now take each phrase and change it into a rule using the word 'must . . .'; for example, 'We act as if each office is an island which has no interaction with any other office', becomes 'Each office must behave like an island with no interaction with any other office'. Keep going until you have identified all the perverse 'rules' people are currently abiding by. (Take a moment to have a laugh at them!) Now reverse each 'rule' into its opposite; for example, 'Each office must act like an island' becomes 'Each office must interact with other offices on a regular basis'. Keep going until you have a list of 'good' rules.

Have another go at distilling your two lists of 'good' rules into a few primary drivers of your business. Now brainstorm what needs to be done to ensure these rules are kept. For example, ensure that nothing contradicts the rules you have identified, such as in your performance management systems, reporting requirements or organization structure. Address any obstacles. Then release people to act within the guiding framework of these rules.

2. Structures for flocking

To what extent are your organization structures getting in the way of 'flocking'? How can they be adapted to increase your organization's responsiveness to shifts in the marketplace? How can structures be freed up to encourage self-organization?

Use the following checklist of questions to assess your potential to restructure:

1. What is your current organization structure based on? Supply or demand? For example, are you functionally organized (i.e. supply driven) or organized around customer groups (i.e. demand driven)? How could you organize more around demand?

2. How are competitors organized? How are other comparable industries organized? Could you try any of these alternatives? With what benefit? Is there any organization structure that no one else has tried? What could it do for you?

3. Reflect on the last major shift in your market. How long did it take you to respond to it? What was the main constraint? Is it still a constraint? And what would it take to remove that constraint?

4. How quickly can people move from one assignment to the next? How many steps are needed to reassign someone? How many people need to be involved? Take decisions? What can be done to reduce the number of steps? What can be done to reduce the number of people involved? What would it take to reduce it to zero? With what benefit?

5. How long does it take to reassign assets? How does this time period compare to shifts in your marketplace? Longer? Shorter? If longer, what can be done to shorten the time taken? What would it take to reduce this time to zero? With what benefit?

3. Identifying hidden redundancy: the leverage point exercise

One of the keys to freeing-up resources is knowing which resources are committed to high-value activities and where to reposition those that are not.

Chris Edwards and Mel Scott of Cranfield Business School developed the following model for identifying ways to maximize competitive advantage. This tool will help you to free up your best people so that they can prepare for uncertain futures, and enable you to respond creatively when the situation demands.

To be successful in this exercise, it is essential to be clear about the purpose of the business or individual team in question.

(a) What is my core purpose?

First, use the chunking up tools from Chapter 2. Take the product or output of your business/team and ask: 'What does that achieve for the customer?' Take the answer to this question and continue to chunk up. Make sure that your answers are about delivering value to customers. Come to a conclusion about your purpose. Make sure that this purpose gives you competitive advantage in terms of meeting your customers' needs.

This exercise is equally valid for those with internal rather than external customers. If you are examining what you deliver to internal customers, start by looking at your customer's external clients, and consider how your output ultimately contributes to meeting the external clients' needs. It may add to your understanding of the potential value you provide to your firm.

(b) Identifying core activities

Discuss and decide on content for the four categories shown in Figure 3.1 relative to the purpose you have identified.

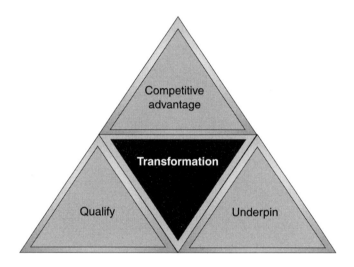

Figure 3.1 *Capability triangle*

(i)   Underpin. List all the activities that underpin what you do in the organization. This includes all supporting activities, such as administration, and all infrastructure such as property, systems, etc.

(ii)   Qualify. List all the activities that you believe are necessary to qualify you to be considered by your customers as potential vendors. What do you have to do for your potential customers even to consider you in comparison to your competitors?

(iii) Competitive advantage. List the activities that provide your product/ service with a competitive advantage within your marketplace. Why do people buy your product or service over those of your competitors?

If you do not have a competitive advantage, list the qualities of the product/service that does and what activities you would need to under-take to deliver those qualities.

(iv) Transformation. What would it take to transform your offerings to the market? (See Figure 3.2 for the cycle of advantage.) If there is serious competition in your market, other organizations will be seeking to acquire the qualities that give you competitive advantage. Very soon your customers will accept these standards as the norm and these qual-ities will become qualifiers for entry into the marketplace. You will therefore need to seek new ways to achieve competitive advantage. What can you do that will transform the product or service and give you competitive advantage for years to come?

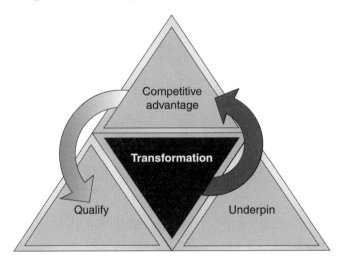

Figure 3.2 *The cycle of advantage*

(c) Leverage points

Take the activities that you listed under the above headings and put them on four flip charts with three columns against each activity (Figure 3.3). Put ticks against the activities that:

- support sustainable competitive advantage;
- benchmark well against competitors and external suppliers;
- are a core business activity (from the customer's point of view).

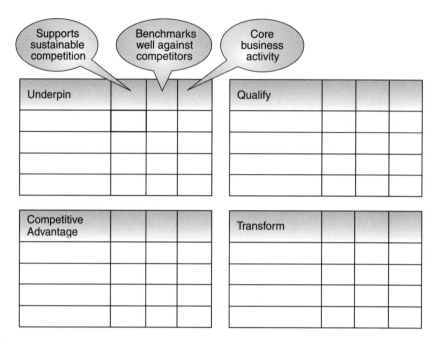

Figure 3.3 *Leverage points*

(d) Homing in

Take the charts and look at the lines with the least number of ticks. Are these areas taking up time and attention? Could people be better employed elsewhere? How could you:

- Simplify this activity?
- Eliminate this activity?
- Outsource it?
- Forget it?

Look at activities with the most number of ticks. What could you achieve with more time and attention allocated to them? Where could extra resource add most value?

Redeploy your team accordingly.

The same exercise can be conducted for physical assets or any other invested resource. For example, where is your current IT spend? Does it contribute to areas of high or low impact? Underpinning or transformational activities?

For more resources on freeing-up resources, see www.AlphaLeaders.com

Conclusion

Anticipation requires sensory systems able to detect weak signals, leaders with the mental agility to understand them, and organizations with the flexibility to respond to them. But it is only one of the three qualities leaders and organizations need, if they are to meet today's business challenges successfully. In the following three chapters, we will tackle the second element of Alpha Leadership: Alignment.

References

1. Reynolds, C. (1987) *Flocks, Herds, and Schools: A Distributed Behavioral Model.* In *Computer Graphics,* **21**(4), 25–34, SIGGRAPH 1987 Conference Proceedings. See also the animation of birds flocking at http://www.red3d.com/cwr/boids/applet/.
2. Bonabeau, E. and Theraulaz, G. (2000) Swarm smarts, *Scientific American,* March.
3. Harris, L. (1998) Awareness, Usage and Opinions of Major Management Consultancy Firms, survey, July.
4. James, S. (2001) *The Business-As-Usual Culture and Its Road to Repeated Failure,* presented at PMI conference.
5. Kolind, L. (1996) told to *Fast Company,* June-July.
6. Kelly, K. (1997) New Rules for the New Economy, *Wired,* September.
7. Barker, J. and Bukan, W. (n.d.) *Paradigm Prisms,* video workshops, see http://www.joelbarker.com.

Part II

Align

*In the quantum world, relationships are not just interesting
. . . they are all there is to reality.*

Margaret Wheatley

The essential message of Part II is that the good leader inspires people to act because they want to, not because they have to. Effort, creativity, problem solving and determination given freely by people are the foundation of a high performing team. Weak leaders instruct people to do a job; strong leaders get much more out of people by dovetailing each individual's self-interest with the team's and the organization's goals.

Having adopted the principles we talked about in Part I, you have an efficient and sensitive sensory system capable of detecting the 'weak signals' that warn you of emerging opportunities and potential dangers. You have increased your mental agility so that you can shape the future and make the most of the opportunities that offer themselves. You have liberated your resources from the constraints of hidebound and rigid organization, so that they can organize themselves and 'flock' to or 'swarm' around the projects and focal points that are the seeds of future success.

You have, in short, endowed the organization with the ability to anticipate events. This gives you a valuable competitive advantage, but before you can exploit it, you need to 'align' the organization. This is the theme of Part II.

Effective alignment operates on three levels: the leader's ability to embody his or her goals; alignment of the relationships and coalitions among people in teams that get the job done; and the wider alignment of the organization's culture to its goals.

Leading through embodiment starts with the alignment of what you value and how you spend your life, whether at work or at home. Personal alignment is probably the single most effective remedy for stress and dissatisfaction in the workplace and beyond. A high level of personal alignment gives you the charisma, congruence and vision that will inspire the people in your care to act effectively.

At a team level, strong leaders focus on aligning the relationships and coalitions of people that get the job done, rather than just concentrating on the task itself. Paradoxically, the powerful leader's key tool in getting people to follow is first to understand what other people want and where they want to go. As a leader, your skills in team alignment will help get things done and avoid the frustrations of missed deadlines and inaction.

Finally, we will see how you can develop and nurture 'cultures that can act', that is, organizations that are aligned and enabled to act around agreed goals.

Once again, at the end of each chapter, we will provide you with some tools to help you become more aligned as a leader, to create alignment with others, and to get the whole organization moving in the same direction. Many of the tools in Part I were focused either on the organization or on your thinking skills. In Part II, the subject matter is of a more personal nature, and you will need to be willing to be open and self-reflective to get value from some of these tools. Mobilizing people requires a different level of thinking, and a greater degree of self-reflection, than is required to organize tasks.

As Margaret Wheatley puts it, 'power in organizations is the capacity generated by relationships'.[1]

Reference

1.　Wheatley, M. (1999) *Leadership and the New Science*, Barrett Kochler.

4

Leading Through Embodiment

This above all—to thine own self be true

William Shakespeare

Idaho, 1999. A dun-coloured mustang is plunging and panicking in a small, dusty ring. His head is tied to a post, while a weighted sack is thrown over his back and around his legs. This procedure, known as 'sacking out', will continue for several days, and is designed to get the animal used to feeling something on his back prior to putting a saddle on him for the first time. The next stage is to tie one leg and do more sacking out. When each leg has been tied up in turn, the horse will be saddled and the sacking out continued. Before the horse is ridden for the first time, a 'hackamore' (a bitless bridle) is fitted and a rear leg tied up to prevent him from bucking. The whole process will take at least three weeks, and is known as 'breaking' a young horse to prepare it for its first saddle and rider.

It is hard to describe the fear, pain and misery this process entails. Horses are often injured, and some die, in the breaking process. And yet there is an alternative. Monty Roberts, the American horse whisperer, believed that there must be a better way.[1] During mustang hunting trips to the Nevada desert in his teens, he realized that, although the horse is a 'flight' animal that always runs from danger, it is also a 'herd' animal that fears exclusion. He learned, by studying and experimenting, that there is a language 'spoken' by horses, that with care and attention a human can learn. Using this language, Roberts can win a horse's trust and work with it to accept a saddle and rider with no pain, no fear, and the whole process takes approximately 30 minutes. Yes, *minutes*.

Monty Roberts' training method is modelled on the leadership style of the lead mare. He picks his environment carefully – a small circular ring in which he can stand in the centre so that even when the horse runs away it is never far. When a horse is brought into the ring to be 'started' (a more accurate description than 'broken'), it quite naturally wants to run away. Roberts lets the horse flee, and in fact encourages it to do so: he sends the horse away from him, using non-verbal signals that drive the horse away at a calm, steady pace. The horse is sensitive to relationship messages, and soon catches on that the horse whisperer is behaving like a parent, and isn't actually going to hurt him. It feels safe enough to open negotiations.

Through painstaking observation, Roberts learned that an ear cocked in the handler's direction means 'I'm ready to negotiate'; that a licking and chewing motion means 'We can come to an agreement'; and that when a horse drops its head and runs with its nose close to the ground, it is saying 'I understand and trust you, and will do what you ask'.

Finally the horse signals 'I am ready to submit if you stop chasing me', and in response the horse whisperer comes to a halt and turns his back. The horse then fulfils its part of the bargain and walks up, like a repentant teenager, and gently puts its nose on the horse whisperer's shoulder, as it would do with the lead mare. Roberts calls this process 'join-up'.

The next stage is to turn a temporary truce into a leader–follower relationship. The horse whisperer begins to walk slowly away from the horse, and the horse has to decide whether to follow or to stay put. The horse is asking itself questions like: Where is this person going? Is it worth going there too? Will I be safer with him or safer here?

One key to success is the manner in which the horse whisperer walks. A horse is more likely to follow someone who has a confident step and seems to know where he or she is going. In the wild, the horse's chances of survival are low on its own. However, if the lead mare isn't sure where she is going, being in the herd isn't safe either. Just like humans, horses assess the confidence and self-assurance of their leaders using non-verbal signals. If the horse is confident in the horse whisperer, it will begin to follow him or her around the ring – and 'follow-up' has been achieved.

Once join-up and follow-up have been established, the rest is easy. The horse feels safe with its new leader, enjoys the relationship, likes the games and tasks it is being trained to do, isn't quite sure of the final outcome, but is happy to cooperate in the process.

Monty Roberts' approach to starting young horses is a powerful contrast to traditional methods. His approach is also a pertinent analogy for new approaches to human leadership. This is not a case of simply 'walking the talk': this is an example of someone who lives, thinks and breathes his beliefs.

This is what we mean by 'leading through embodiment': Roberts' goals are so intrinsic to him that everything he says and does is in step with them – he is congruent at every level of his being. The work he chooses to do is absolutely consistent with what he believes, and further adds to his expertise and his ability to act out his beliefs. Finally, he embodies his beliefs and goals so fully that, paradoxically, he is able to step beyond them and inhabit the world of others.

These three core principles in his approach are useful indicators that we can apply in learning how to lead through embodiment in a business context: personal alignment, choice of work content and the interplay of expertise and learning, and the ability to see the world through someone else's eyes.

Successful horse whispering starts with a strong sense of your own values, and an alignment between what you believe and how you act. Roberts has an extraordinary sense of purpose. As he puts it: 'I am on a mission' – a mission to make the world a better place for horses. Every action he takes is entirely consistent with this central mission and with his core beliefs. This deep alignment gives confidence, and the ability to walk 'like you know where you are going', which inspires 'follow-up'. In Monty Roberts' case, it has also allowed him to stick to his revolutionary approach in the face of ferocious criticism from the community of traditional horse trainers.

The second core principle is choosing to be 'hands on' in applying expertise, while maintaining a curiosity and desire to learn that will further enable the expert to act in accordance with his or her beliefs. Kelly Marks, a close associate of Roberts, and the only person who is accredited to teach his methods, is a remarkable example of this. She remains a 'hands on' practitioner – spending hours with students demonstrating and training the techniques. Her knowledge of horsemanship is so strong and so deeply ingrained that it is second nature to her. She has the expertise to walk fearlessly into a small ring with half a ton of bucking and rearing horse, and yet still retains a humbleness and desire to learn from others that leads her into new fields of endeavour; for example, working with Manchester Business School to apply the principles of 'join-up' to leadership practice in organizations.

Third, it is essential to be able to see the world through someone else's eyes, whether that be horse or person, so that your interaction with them starts from their point of view and not your own. It is noteworthy that Roberts started by observing and learning the language of horses, rather than by insisting that they adopt his. With this perspective, it becomes clear that problems really can be part of the solution. By truly understanding a horse's – or person's – position, actions that appear detrimental to achieving a goal may be seen as a way forward. For example, the horse wants to run away. The traditional approach is to get a rope around the horse's neck and hang on to it for dear life. Roberts' approach is startling in that he goes with what the animal wants rather than against it, saying to the animal: 'You want to go away? Then really go away, and keep going until you are ready to come back to me.'

We will explore these themes in the following pages, and will conclude with a selection of tools that will help you to enhance your sense of personal alignment, to balance your work content, and to improve your ability to see the world from points of view other than your own.

Personal alignment

A leader's internal congruence or alignment is a powerful agent in moving people from words to action. Leaders who know who they are, know their 'calling', and walk their talk, will be trusted and will attract motivated followers.

This leadership quality, called by a variety of names including self-confidence, personal presence, gravitas and charisma, is the behavioural manifestation of deep internal processes. Although behavioural training can increase presence, any lack of authenticity or sincerity is readily detected. Significant change in a leader's alignment needs to be generated at a deeper level than the behavioural to be authentic.

You can only express a vision with feeling and sincerity if you really believe in it and are aligned with it. Try asking yourself a simple question about your job: if these were the last five years of your life, is that what you would be doing? If the answer is a resounding no, then you may want to think about the alignment of what you value and how you spend your working life.

A colleague recently had her first, long-awaited child. She returned to work after only seven days maternity leave. However, she also said to friends that 'What I really want to do is take 18 months out of my career and spend it with my son.' It is too easy, in today's pressured business environment, to lose sight of what matters, to deny what our heart tells us is the right thing to do and to mistake the priorities of the immediate, work-oriented present for those of the long term. Who would want 'I wish I had stayed later at the office' for their epitaph, but how many of us act as if we do?

More than a century ago, Oscar Wilde noticed this phenomenon, writing: 'Man will kill himself by overwork . . . One's regret is that . . . man has been forced into a groove in which he cannot freely develop what is wonderful, and fascinating, and delightful in him – in which, in fact, he misses the true pleasure and joy of living.'[2] When our values and the way we live are in alignment, we can rediscover the wonderful, the fascinating and the delightful in life.

The problem with most business goals is that it can be hard to see how they fit with what really matters to you. As John Higgins of Ashridge Management College puts it, 'Freud never mentioned shareholder value.' The idea that we can hold something like shareholder value at our core is absurd. Our personal identity and purpose cannot reside in this type of objective. We need to dig deeper to find what truly drives us – our 'calling' in life – and then to translate this calling back into our work context. And if we find it impossible to make the two worlds congruent, then a fundamental change is essential.

True personal presence comes from a clear alignment of body, mind, emotions and spirit. For a person to be fully aligned, one's sense of who one is as a person needs to be aligned with one's values and beliefs, reflected in one's core skills and hence into the contexts within which one lives and works.

Our brains, language and social systems are layered and, as we discussed in Chapter 2, we move between layers of meaning and significance by chunking up and down. Leaders need to have some kind of layered model in their minds as they seek personal alignment. A system of 'logical levels' is a useful way of exploring the dimensions on which we can attain alignment.[3]

The six levels are:

1. What I am a part of – context, self-transcendence, spirit.
2. Who I am – identity.
3. What I believe – beliefs, values, motivations.
4. What I am capable of – skills, competencies, ambition.

5. What I do – behaviour, actions.
6. The environment – external surroundings.

Each level synthesizes, organizes and directs the levels immediately below it. Building the pyramid from the bottom up, we can say that our environment or physical context consists of the circumstances in which we behave; that how we behave is based on what we believe ourselves capable of and what we want to do with that ability; that our ambitions and capabilities are shaped by our values and beliefs; that our values and beliefs both generate and are derived from our sense of self; and that, whether we recognize it or not, most of us have a sense of self-transcendence – a feeling of being part of something that reaches beyond our individual lives.

Powerful leaders are fully aligned on every level. Unfortunately, it is easy to get out of alignment on any one of these levels, and as a result to experience stress, anxiety and a feeling that what we are doing lacks meaning. We can ignore these incongruities, often for many years, but they will eventually take their toll on our motivation, our energy, and even our health.

Context

Aligned leaders have a sense of something greater than themselves or their company – they feel a part of a larger story. This could be a humanistic vision, such as helping people work together to develop humanity and fulfil our potential as a species; it could be a vision of the potential contribution they can make to the development of technology or to society; sometimes it is a spiritual or religious sense that life is about caring for one another. Whatever your view of what life is about, it will affect how you live your life day-to-day. The more that others can relate to your vision, the greater your leadership potential will be. Nelson Mandela was able to change South Africa from the confines of a prison cell because of his unwavering sense of his place in history.

Disconnects between our context and what we do can be profoundly disturbing; for instance, people who believe that humanity is part of a planetary organism James Lovelock has christened 'Gaia' will feel deeply uncomfortable in organizations that emit excessive greenhouse gases; leaders who believe we need to care for others will find it hard to remain aligned with an organization that has announced massive job cuts. If business circumstances make job cuts inevitable, and your organization depends on people who care about people, treat the people you make redundant with as much care, compassion and dignity as you can muster.

Identity

Aligned leaders have a high degree of self-awareness and self-acceptance, yet are also motivated to achieve more and to improve their skills.

They are at ease with their personal, social and cultural history – how they have come to be who they are. As the leader matures, he or she may need to modify the influence of his or her personal history without being at odds with it: for example, the authors have worked with leaders who have had to overcome difficulties imposed both by affluent and deprived backgrounds, or difficulties resulting from being part of an ethnic or cultural minority group, or a majority group. Most leaders know theoretically that a lack of understanding of the richness of human culture, of diversity, can restrict their effectiveness. It is another thing to look at themselves with candour and understand how their background enhances and detracts from their leadership roles.

Aligned leaders need to have come to terms with their current roles in life: work, home, social and leisure. They need to feel good about their place in the world, and have come to terms with the hand that destiny has dealt them. Not all our dreams come true, and learning to deal with disappointment effectively enables a robust sense of identity: leaders need to be comfortable with their seniority in the organization, or lack thereof; their educational accomplishments or otherwise; their family situation or single status; their children or their fertile imagination.

Alpha leaders are oriented towards the future – they can take disappointment and turn it into hope for the future, while at the same time coming to terms with who they are in the present.

In addition to self-acceptance in terms of personal history and present circumstances, Alpha leaders have a clear sense of who they are becoming in the future. They will have a sense of their mission or calling – the special contribution they can make to the world and the legacy they would like to leave behind. In just the same way that an organization should have a clear purpose extrapolated from its key competencies, so an individual leader should understand what his or her special contribution can be and seek to maximize it. When someone is aiming to be the very best he or she can be, other people want to share the excitement. Just as a company is enhanced by a powerful vision, what Collins and Porras call a BHAG (big hairy audacious goal),[4] the life of an individual is also enhanced by having a powerful vision of what he or she wants to create.

In a practical, go-getting world where bottom line is the measure of success, it may seem 'a bit deep' to ask, 'Who are you? Where have you come from? Where are you going?' Nevertheless, the alignment of your sense of identity with your most deeply held values and the way you behave is key to leadership charisma and your ability to influence.

Values and beliefs

Because Alpha leaders want to harness the discretionary energy of people, getting them to do things because they want to rather than because they have to, Alpha leaders attempt to 'walk their talk' as best they can. They tend to be more aware than others of their values and beliefs, and make efforts to reflect these in their behaviour. It is the congruence between identity, beliefs and behaviour that we call 'charisma'. It inspires profound trust in those who work with us.

Our beliefs about ourselves can also be profoundly undermining. Almost without noticing, during the course of our lives we take on board what other people say about us – you're always late, you don't stick at things, you're careless, inconsiderate – and before we know it, it seems as if they form part of our fundamental self. It may take some work to separate the features of yourself that are really your essence from those that are merely the products of frequently repeated beliefs about yourself.

(A brief aside: try completing the following phrase 'I'm too . . .'. We guarantee that 90% of our female readers will come up with the sentence 'I'm too fat', regardless of their absolute weight or size. Beliefs about ourselves can be insidious.)

Capabilities

Aligned leaders have a unique sense of mission, that is supported by their beliefs and values, and is delivered to the world by their skills and competencies. Essential leadership skills vary from situation to situation, but skills that seem generic to most situations are the ability to develop vision and strategy, and to implement them; the ability to influence and manage relationships; the ability to appoint excellent direct reports, and to coach and delegate appropriately; and the ability to prioritize. Business is so complex that no leader can be conspicuously good at every aspect of their role. But great leaders are conspicuously good at finding other competent people to delegate tasks to, and they take responsibility for ensuring that the organization maintains a full repertoire of necessary capabilities.

Behaviour

Aligned leaders know that, because of their visible position, their behaviour is watched closely, and exerts a disproportionate influence on the behaviour of others. They take care to ensure that how they act matches what they say they believe. This is perhaps the level that falls into misalignment most easily; for example, how often have managers said that people come first, or that training is the lifeblood of the company, only to axe both when times get tough?

Aligned leaders use the visibility of their behaviour to transmit messages to, and manage the perceptions of bosses, peers, subordinates and other key stakeholders.

Environment

Aligned leaders are skilful managers of ambiences and environments. They deliberately design their own work environments to promote their values and priorities, and take great pains to ensure that important meetings are held at times, in places and under circumstances that will make them productive. Environmental alignment is often overlooked, and yet is easy to address with powerful consequences. For example, when mentoring members of your team and wanting them to internalize some tough messages from you, do you sit across from them, behind your desk and its myriad papers? Or do you sit at right angles to them, inviting their openness to you, at a clear desk that demonstrates the focus of your attention?

One young CEO, who had inherited the business from his father, said in coaching sessions that he felt as if his father was constantly looking over his shoulder, criticizing him. This feeling was undermining his ability to grow the company with new strategies and products. On visiting the CEO's office, his coach discovered that no changes had been made to the office since his father had left the firm. The coach was amused to see the walls covered with photos of the CEO's father, taken at various landmark occasions for the company, and in full view when he sat at his desk. No wonder his father's presence felt overwhelming. One small, simple step to relieving his situation was to change the décor!

When starting a horse, Monty Roberts demonstrates alignment across all of these levels of leadership. As a person, he is at ease with himself, certain of the contribution he is making to the lives of horses. He knows the value of the legacy he will leave behind him. He wears his values and beliefs on his sleeve, and has developed his skills and abilities to promote them. His behaviour is integral to his method, and he has honed it to such a level that he can make a horse run faster or slower simply by spreading his fingers or moving the focus of his eyes from one part of the horse's body to another. He is a masterly manager of the environment, and can quickly discover what aspects of the horse's environment are causing it to behave in a particular way.

Our challenge is to achieve this degree of alignment in order to be truly effective business leaders.

The expert who learns

To be respected, trusted and followed, leaders must be perceived as qualified to lead. The more knowledge-intensive the business, and the more that people are left to manage themselves, the more important becomes the leader's own professional expertise. Content is key – in the knowledge economy, knowledge is the currency. As we move towards an economy in which all aspects of it are driven by the connectivity of information, where every worker is a knowledge worker, this requirement to display deep personal competence and expertise will become ever more prominent.

Scientific research teams give us a useful preview of what the future is likely to hold in all aspects of business since they consist of able, highly motivated individuals trading in pure knowledge. They are a microcosm, and in many ways the prototype, of the knowledge-based partnerships widely predicted to become the dominant business life-form.

In her unpublished doctoral thesis, Rose Trevelyan described the leadership styles in two scientific research teams.[5] In terms of performance, the differences between the teams was marked: Team A, led by George, scored 2.7 in terms of frequency and impact of publications; Team B, led by Alice, scored 4.9, and in addition rated much higher in terms of reported job satisfaction. The leadership styles of the two team leaders was fundamentally different. George had an excellent track record in his discipline, but had stopped doing his own research 10 years previously. He saw his role as securing funding for the team, and acting as communication controller. In striking contrast, Alice was still very involved in her own research. She spent a great deal of time sitting at the bench alongside her team members, who both admired and respected her.

This vignette has some challenging implications. If it indeed presages the way organizations will require their leaders to act in future, it demands that we ask ourselves some awkward questions. If you lead a sales organization, when was the last time you made a sale? If you are CEO of a consulting firm, when was the last time you solved a client problem or rolled your sleeves up to prepare a presentation? If you are director of nursing, who was the last patient you cared for?

It is all too easy for general managers who are not expert in the products of their division to play a hands-off supervisory role. Supervising on behalf of head office, or being the corporate voice, or even doing cost control and balancing the books, is not sufficient to give credibility. The leader's contribution must be meaningful to the followers themselves, and demonstrate at some level a high degree of expertise.

In other words, it is essential to invest a significant proportion of your time in 'own work' (that is, hands-on work that leads to an outcome created by you personally), compared to time spent supervising the work of others. We have a feeling that the shift towards own work will become ever more important in business. Is Bill Gates's dual title of chairman and chief software architect the start of a trend?

However, there is a paradox here. We need to be sufficiently expert to be comfortable enough to let go of this expert role; to be curious, to question, observe and learn. Being an expert, doing our own work well, can get in our way if we are not careful. We need to find what Bill Isaacs calls a 'second innocence'[6] – a learning stance that is made possible by what we know, but is not impeded by it.

Ashridge Management College consultant John Higgins' work with improvisational actors at the Comedy Store in London provides a helpful analogy. The actors' confidence in their professional expertise allows them to relax in their uniquely highly charged, high-pressure environment. It provides them with the stability from which they become more curious, more able to explore leads and avenues thrown to them by their colleagues. One of the team, Neil Mullarkey, added the comment, 'It doesn't feel like work.' If only all our work experience felt like that!

Second position first

Personal alignment is about being clear who you are and where you want to go. 'Own work' and continuous learning is about making sure you add value. But if you haven't got anyone to come with you, it cannot be called leadership. Leadership involves at least two parties: the individual who takes on the role of the leader and one or more individuals who are willing to follow.

It is important to note the paradox here. Leaders need to be very clear in themselves about where they are going, and what they want. From this strength of character and purpose, the leader then needs to give up her own viewpoint to step temporarily into the world of the people she wants to lead.

Judith Lowe, Pace Personal Development's training director, calls this approach 'the antidote for mind-reading'. We believe we know where people are coming from without much effort, and interpret their actions and words according to our own set of beliefs and values – in other words, we try to mind-read. It is so easy to believe that the way we see the world is the 'right' way, the truth, and that anyone who thinks differently is just plain wrong; that any interpretation of a dialogue other than our own is obviously wrong because the other person has a poor memory, poor hearing or is terminally stupid. But as Murray Anderson-Wallace of consultancy Inter-logics says, 'In any dialogue we can only own 50% of the meaning.' In order to see things from someone else's position, we have to step into their space, leaving our own temporarily behind.

There are several 'perceptual positions' from which an interaction may be viewed. Perceptual positions refer to the fundamental points of view one can take concerning the relationship between oneself and another person. One way to understand people better when you are interacting with them is to adopt these positions in turn. Such shifts in the positions from which we consider a situation can greatly enrich our perceptions of that situation and improve our ability to influence it.

There are four perceptual positions:[7]

- *1st position.* Your own point of view, beliefs and assumptions, seeing the external world through your own eyes – an 'I' position.
- *2nd position.* Another person's point of view, beliefs and assumptions, seeing the external world through his or her eyes – a 'you' position.
- *3rd position.* A point of view outside of the relationship between yourself and the other person – a 'they' position.
- *4th position.* The perspective of the whole system – a 'we' position.

The first position is our usual stance, focusing exclusively on what we see, hear, feel and think. The second position requires us to try on for size how someone else sees, hears, feels and thinks – paying attention to their specific experience and context. The third position requires us to step back from the interaction between 'me' and 'you', in an attempt to see it from the point of view of an independent observer. What would someone notice happening? What would they see, hear? What conclusions would they draw? Finally, the fourth position draws each of these viewpoints together and examines the interaction from the perspective of all.

Each of these positions will lead to very different interpretations of what is going on. It is useful to pay attention to those differences when stepping back into first position, and reflecting on what this tells you about an effective way forward.

This may seem easy, but child psychologist Jean Piaget maintained that our ability to decentre (to see the world from someone else's point of view) is not innate, and in fact doesn't properly emerge until we are four or five years old. Our decentring skills need to be honed throughout our lives, if we are to be truly effective leaders.

Tools for thought

1. Gaining personal alignment

The following exercise is designed to help you analyse the extent to which you are effectively aligned, to identify where you need to align yourself more fully, and to help you begin to think about what changes you want to make.

One early reader of the manuscript of this book commented: 'This exercise would take me two years to complete!' Actually, this is probably an underestimate. Thinking about, exploring and enhancing one's internal alignment is a lifetime's work. Every time we ask these questions or repeat this exercise, new insights emerge.

Depending on the amount of time you have available, you can do this exercise quickly as a 10-minute sketch that you can revisit another day, or you can take a whole afternoon thinking it through. One useful tip is that revisiting this exercise several times will deepen your experience of it, and give you a chance to ponder on the questions over a longer period of time.

To get value from this exercise, a degree of openness and willingness to be self-reflective will be required. If your mood today is for action rather than the introspective processes of alignment, we suggest you come back to it at another time.

(a) Understanding your levels

Take time to answer the following questions. Use a brainstorming style and jot down your answers to each question as a stream of consciousness, as if you were writing in a personal journal.

Alternatively you could talk the questions through with a friend, or someone with good listening skills, or coaching or counselling experience. It might be useful to find someone else who is reading this book and go through the exercise together.

Of course, you are a complex, dynamic person and your notes from this exercise are simply a snapshot of you at one moment in time.

Environment: Think about your current working environment. Imagine the place where your desk or office is. What does it look like? What can you see from where you sit? What noises do you hear? Does the place smell of the air conditioning, carpets or plants? How do you feel, when sitting at your desk? What is the atmosphere like around you? Think also of the various places you go during your workday, and include all these different places and environments as part of this reflection.

Behaviours: What do you do, on a daily basis? How much time do you spend thinking or planning? How much time do you spend talking to people face to face and on the phone, and dealing with e-mails and voice-mails? How much time do you spend in meetings? Are your meetings constructive in that they move things forward, creative in that they produce useful ideas or supportive in that they allow you to help colleagues test and develop their ideas? Are these meetings one-on-one, or in groups? Think about all the ways you behave in the course of your working week. How do you do things? And what does this say about you?

Capabilities: What are your strengths? Which of your skills influence your behaviour? What do you emphasize because you are good at it? What do you avoid because you feel it is a weakness? Are your main skills technical, inter-personal or inspirational? How would you rate your strategic and planning skills? Think about the abilities you use on a day-to-day basis, and describe and assess them.

Values and beliefs: What are your own personal values? What do you value about yourself? What do you care about most? Which of your own skills and qualities do you value most? What do you value most in other people: integrity, authenticity, a determination to do their best, high performance?

What are your beliefs about yourself? What are you good at? What are you poor at? What are you like as a person? Which of your beliefs are help-ful in your work, or support what you do, and which of them are unhelpful in your work, or undermine what you do? Be as diligent in your descriptions of the latter beliefs as the former.

What do you believe about your competence and ability in general? How good are you at different things, and how good are you overall at what you do?

Identity: Who are you, in terms of your upbringing and socio-economic background, and in terms of your experience as a sibling or an only child? Who are you now as an adult? What are your roles at work, at home, among your friends and in your local community? What are your aspirations? Who will you be in the future, and who would you like to be?

Imagine yourself in your healthy old age looking back on your life. Ask yourself who you have been, what has been important and what do you value most about the life you have lived? If, aged 80, you felt you had ful-filled your potential, what would you have done, what would you be like and what would you now be exploring?

What will you leave behind you? What will be your unique contribution to the world? What is special about what you can do with your life?

Context: Do you believe in something spiritual, or do you believe life was a cosmic accident? Your spiritual vision might be theistic or humanistic. You might believe in humanity's ability to make the world a nicer place to live in, or you might believe that it is every man for himself in a natural world red in tooth and claw.

Whatever your view, think about it and describe it. What you believe about life and its meaning, or lack of it, will guide your behaviour, and help to shape your other beliefs, your sense of self, your values and, ultimately, your abilities and behaviours.

(b) Summarizing your development areas

Draw up a table like the one shown in Table 4.1, inserting your answers to each of the questions in the columns headed 'Strengths' and 'Development areas'.

(c) Moving to action

- Summarize the strengths, at each level, which support your leadership ability.
- Summarize the development areas, at each level, that may undermine your leadership ability.
- Think of what you can do to increase your strengths and reduce your weaknesses.
- Look for any ways in which the levels are not aligned with each other: for example, does your behaviour align with your values? Are there gaps which affect the congruence of either your behaviour or your sense of identity? Is your environment congruent with your values?
- Identify steps to improve alignment.

It would take another book to discuss fully the kinds of things one can do at each level to improve oneself and one's alignment. In some cases it is

Table 4.1   *Actions to build personal alignment*

	Strengths	Development areas	What can I do about it?
Environment	What are the good things about my environment? What works for me? What works for other people?	What are the unpleasant things? What doesn't work for me? What doesn't work for other people?	
Behaviour	What do I do that works? That achieves my objectives?	What do I do that doesn't work? That doesn't achieve my objectives?	
Capabilities	What are my strong skills?	Which skills do I lack?	
Beliefs and values	What values do I have that support who I am and where I am going? What beliefs do I have that make me stronger?	What values do I have that interfere with who I am and where I am going? What beliefs undermine me?	
Identity	What are the helpful things about my sense of identity?	What are the things about who I am that I feel undermine me? How can I turn these elements of my identity to my advantage?	
Spiritual	What are the benefits of my sense of meaning in life?	What are the disadvantages of my sense of meaning in life?	

quite obvious what you need to do, and it only remains for you to do it. In other cases some thought is needed, and it might be useful to discuss your self-assessment with a close friend or a trusted colleague. Occasionally, particularly when the issue is deep within you, you will feel the need for expert advice and you should seek out a professional consultant, executive coach or some other qualified counsellor.

2. Concentric circles exercise: balancing expertise

Leadership can be viewed as a unique set of skills that complements other competence and expertise. Viewed from this perspective, leadership provides *added value* to fundamental technical ability and expertise (Figure 4.1). In other words, strengthening leadership ability can help any manager to improve his or her capacity to achieve results.

Figure 4.1   *Balancing expertise*

The most effective leaders are typically those who are anchoring leadership ability to a strong foundation of technical expertise. While in some situations it is possible to succeed on strong leadership ability with very little technical competence, this is not usually the optimal combination. It would be a bit like a good soccer coach attempting to lead a tennis team. There would be some overlaps, but there would also be significant differences in some areas.

The ratio of technical competence to leadership ability required for success depends to some degree on the role an individual has within the system or organization. To continue the sports analogy, the players on a sports team must have specific competence and expertise in their positions to be effective. It is more important for the coach, on the other hand, to possess effective leadership ability (Figure 4.2).

The concentric circles in the Figures can be seen as a map of leadership capabilities. The inner circle represents technical competence, and the outer ring represents leadership. Both are necessary, but neither is sufficient.

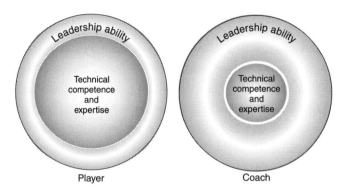

Figure 4.2 *Different ratios, different roles*

When the outer ring is too narrow the leader gets lost in the detail, and you end up with constant meddling and micro-management. But if the circle (representing the leader's technical competence) is too small, you end up with an uninformed, 'hit and miss' kind of leadership based on whim, rather than on intuitions about the strategic priorities derived from an understanding of the tactical details.

You can apply the concentric circles to individual leaders. Former American President Ronald Reagan, for example, was a 'small core' leader. He was not well-endowed with technical competence (that was provided by his advisers), but his leadership 'ring' was substantial. Steve Jobs, at Apple, was also a 'small core' leader, but he had in Steve Wozniak a 'large core' co-leader.

What kind of leader are you? If you are a 'details' person who tends to lack the 'big picture', your leadership 'ring' is probably too narrow and you should delegate more while working to build your broader leadership capabilities. If you are a 'vision' person who tends to miss technical detail, relying instead on intuition, your competence 'core' is probably too small, and you should get more involved in the details, in the guts of the business.

The difficulty of reconciling both vision and detail in one individual favours the leadership pair, such as Jobs and Wozniak, Jobs and Cook, Hewlett and Packard, and, more generally, the chief executive officer (CEO) and the chief operating officer (COO).

Look around at your fellow managers. What 'rings' do they inhabit? Is there a complementary manager who could fill the gaps you perceive in your style? How could you team more effectively?

3. Perceptual positions exercise

Perceptual positions are characterized and expressed by key words: 'I', 'you', 'they' and 'we'. These key words are a type of 'meta message' that can help you to recognize and direct the perceptual positions people are assuming during a particular interaction. For instance, someone who frequently uses the word 'I' is more likely to be speaking from his or her point of view than a person who is using the word 'we' when talking about ideas or suggestions. A person who is stuck in one perspective can be led to shift perceptual positions through the subtle use of language cues.

For example, let's say a member of a project team is being overly critical of an idea or plan and says something like, 'I don't think this will ever work', indicating a strong 'first position' reaction. The team leader has a number of options to guide the individual to a different point of view.

- To encourage a more systemic position, try saying, 'I understand you have some big concerns about this plan. How do you think we can approach it in a way that will work?'
- To guide the person to an observer position, try suggesting, 'Imagine you were a consultant for this team. What ways would you suggest for them to work together more effectively?'
- To encourage the critical individual to go to 'second position', say: 'Put yourself in my shoes [or one of the other team members'] for a moment. What reactions do you think I would have to your concern?'

One of the most important communication skills for leaders is the ability to switch their points of view, to generate many different perspectives of a situation or experience. Practice the following steps to adopt different perceptual positions:

1. Think about a challenging situation you have been in, or are expecting to be in, involving a particular collaborator. Put yourself fully into first position by imagining that your collaborator is here right now, and that you are looking at him or her through your own eyes.
2. Now imagine you are 'in the shoes' of your collaborator, looking at yourself through his or her eyes. Assume the perspective, beliefs and assumptions of the collaborator as if you were that person for a moment.

3. Now view the relationship between yourself and your collaborator as if you were an observer watching a video of those interactions.

4. As a final experiment, take the perspective of the whole system and consider what would be in the best interest of the system.

Notice how taking the different perceptual positions changes your experience of the interaction. What new awareness did you get about yourself, your collaborator or the situation? What will you do differently as a result?

For more resources on leading through embodiment, see www.AlphaLeaders.com

Conclusion

The ability of leaders, as individuals, to help 'align' their organizations behind a purpose is determined by who they seem to be, what they do and how they do it, and the extent to which they empathize with others.

Authentic, 'together' personalities, who seem to be at peace with themselves and with their leadership roles, are the sort of personalities people find attractive and are inclined to follow. But actions speak louder than first impressions. The leader's work and the way it is done also contribute to the willingness of others to follow. People need to believe they are being led by someone who is able and knows what he or she is doing. And they also need to know that their roles, abilities, personalities and aspirations are understood and respected by their leader and taken into account when tasks and responsibilities are assigned.

In Chapter 5, we will look at ways to achieve alignment and build coalitions among people to get the job done.

References

1. Roberts, M. (1996) *The Man Who Listens to Horses*, Hutchinson. See also www.intelligenthorsemanship.co.uk for details of Kelly Marks and Monty Roberts' demonstrations and training courses.
2. Wilde, O. (1986) *De Profundis and Other Writings*, Penguin Classics.
3. Dilts, R. and Epstein, T. (1989) *NLP Master Practitioner Booklet*, The Dynamic Learning Center.
4. Collins, J. and Porras, J. (1994) *Built to Last: Successful Habits of Visionary Companies*, Harper Business.
5. Trevelyan, R. (1996) Leadership and work attitudes in academic biochemical research groups, unpublished doctoral thesis, University of London.

6. Isaacs, W. (1999) *Dialogue and the Art of Thinking Together: A Pioneering Approach to Communicating in Business and in Life*, Doubleday Books.
7. Delozier, J. and Grinder, J. (1987) *Turtles All the Way Down: Prerequisites to Personal Genius*, Metamorphous Press.

5

Task Through Relationship

Only connect

E. M. Forster

Nelson Mandela demonstrated that it was possible from the confines of a prison cell to change the course of his country's history, and to some degree that of the world, forever.

He was given a life sentence for his campaign for democracy in South Africa in 1964 at the age of 46, and he remained in prison for nearly 28 years until his release at the age of 71 in 1990. Despite the harsh prison regime and manual labour, he succeeded in creating multiracial democracy in South Africa, and he was elected president a mere four years later in 1994.

The African National Congress was founded in 1912 to fight racial discrimination institutionalized in oppressive laws. There were other ANC leaders campaigning to end apartheid, but it was Mandela who succeeded in building a relationship with the South African government from the confines of his cell. How did he do this? With no official authority and limited ability to communicate with the outside world, how was he able to influence his colleagues in the African National Council, his prison wardens, the prison authorities, the government and the international community to create a climate in which negotiation was possible?

Mandela's leadership of the ANC was based on his inclusive leadership style and the way he combined the powerful use of personal relationship and reasonable argument with the threat of terrorist action against government buildings, but not people. Once imprisoned, he saw one of his first tasks was to make peace with his bigoted and sometimes brutal wardens. In his autobiography *Long Walk to Freedom*,[1] he says: 'We believed that all men, even prison wardens, were capable of change, and we did our utmost to try to sway them.' For example, sometimes he had to do things he didn't like in order to achieve his objectives. On one occasion a warden thought he was being friendly by throwing a sandwich on to the grass near a prisoner as if he were feeding an animal. With a nod from Mandela, the other prisoner accepted the gift, and this self-control enabled them to continue building a relationship with the guard. Mandela wanted to find out about the Afrikaner psychology and culture, so he learned their language and read their literature. As an ANC colleague put it: 'You must understand the mind of the opposing commander.'[2] As a result of understanding the Afrikaner mind, Mandela knew that when the time came, he would know how to negotiate with the Afrikaner government.

Observers noted that Mandela 'had an exceptional ability to make everyone who came into contact with him feel special', radiating unusual warmth and charm,[3] and this made an impression on the prison authorities. In 1981, when the justice minister asked for a report on Mandela, their reply included the following:

- Mandela is exceptionally motivated and maintains a strong idealistic approach.
- He maintains outstanding personal relations, is particularly jovial and always behaves in a friendly and respectful way towards figures of authority.
- He is manipulative, but nevertheless not tactless or [sic] provocative.
- There are no visible signs of bitterness towards the whites, although this may be a fine game of bluff on his part.[4]

It was Mandela's statesmanlike conduct in prison that led the South African government to believe that it could do business with him. Eventually he was smuggled in one night to see the president of South Africa, F.W. de Klerk, for a clandestine meeting. De Klerk concluded that he could work with Mandela and that together they could guide their two parties through the tortuous process of negotiation.

As discussions with the South African government progressed, the international community sent emissaries to meet Mandela in his prison cell and to report back. Their first impression of him was not of a guerrilla fighter, but of a potential head of state. This gave international governments the confidence to pressure South Africa to end apartheid and conduct negotiations.

Under his presidency, there was never any suggestion of vengeance and retribution. He brought all the people of his country – black, white, Asian and coloured – with him in a national programme of reconciliation and constructive action to rebuild his country. He anticipated events, positioned his modest resources to respond very quickly to them, and displayed enormous personal integrity. He demonstrated a political adeptness in turning the warring factions around him into partnerships and coalitions.

It would be naive to think of Mandela as some sort of saint, however. During his long imprisonment he had learnt to control his aggression and to 'think with his brains not his blood', holding in mind the goal of a negotiated victory. De Klerk describes a number of occasions when Mandela showed his bitterness with the people who had been his oppressors and imprisoned him for so many years. Most of the time, however, Mandela adopted the philosophy of 'fixed vision, responsive goals and variable means' (see Chapter 2), looked for the good in people and tried to see things from the other parties' points of view.[5]

The modern, multiracial South Africa, in common with every other modern democracy, has its problems, but without Nelson Mandela and his friends and allies it would not exist.

We have focused in this story on the personal qualities of Nelson Mandela as a communicator and a leader, but we could just as easily have discussed the cooperative relationship between Mandela and de Klerk. Both Mandela and de Klerk knew that they themselves had to break any deadlocks in the negotiation process and that only by working together could they create their vision for a democratic multiracial country. Cooperation between people with opposing agendas can create break-throughs that are much greater than those that any one individual could achieve.

Cooperation is a natural human instinct, and can bring out the best in us. A notable example comes from the trenches of the First World War, where British and German soldiers were trying to survive under horrendous conditions. Some battalions were known to have organized artillery bombardments to occur at the same time and the same place each day, so that soldiers on each side knew when and where to keep their heads down.

Axelrod, in The Evolution of Co-operation,[6] gives another example told by the baseball umpire, Ron Luciano.

Over a period of time I learned to trust certain catchers so much that I actually let them umpire for me on the bad days. The bad days usually followed the good nights. . . . On those days there wasn't much I could do but take two aspirins and call as little as possible. If someone I trusted was catching . . . I'd tell them, 'Look, it's a bad day. You'd better take it for me. If it's a strike, hold your glove in place for an extra second. If it's a ball, throw it right back. And please, don't yell.'

No one I worked with ever took advantage of the situation, and no hitter ever figured out what I was doing. And only once did a pitcher ever complain about a call . . . but I didn't say a word. I was tempted though, really tempted.[7]

If cooperation can emerge between governments and revolutionaries, umpires and catchers, and opposing forces on the battlefield, then imagine what is possible between people who are on the same side. Imagine if the spirit of cooperation were the primary driver at all levels of your organization, between you and your suppliers, and with your customers.

The benefits of a high degree of cooperation are obvious. Nevertheless, an enormous amount of organizational energy is wasted in manoeuvres concerned primarily with competing personal agendas. A good deal of organizational time is spent working out who will rule the roost.

Alpha leaders understand human instincts, and spend a good deal of time creating coalitions of people who are willing to work together to make exciting things happen.

Business leaders sometimes focus so intently on their tasks that they do not see that time spent building a coalition could get the job done more quickly, easily and effectively. Time spent building cooperative relationships to achieve tasks can reduce the overall time and cost of the task itself. In addition, with the support of a coalition, the eventual outcomes are much more likely to be sustained.

Alpha leaders work on the basis that if you look after your relationships, the tasks will look after themselves. Alpha leaders combine this relationship orientation with the prioritization principles that we will talk about in Chapter 7: 80:20 Leadership. Studiously use relationship and coaching skills to recruit and develop your direct reports and staff to the point that if you look after them, they will look after the tasks. You can then get on with the business of aligning key opinion leaders in the rest of the organization behind your strategic objectives.

Drawing on generic communication models, observation of successful leaders and the tales of triumph and disaster we hear in our executive coaching work, we can identify three primary principles that can be applied to aligning relationships in business:

- Start by dovetailing agendas;
- Reach for the positive intention;
- Match first, then lead.

Dovetailing agendas

One well-known financial institution uses 'golden handcuffs' to keep staff motivated. People are paid significantly more than they could earn anywhere else and are encouraged to compete aggressively for titles and status. They are prepared to work from 7 a.m. to 10 p.m., because they are earning so much, and they will be able to retire in their mid-40s. But the price the company pays for their loyalty is very high. Staff members do not believe in their leaders. They see many of the decisions made by their bosses as political in nature and designed to win power or money, and they follow suit. They spend a great deal of their time and energy feathering their own nests; consequently they spend very little time working for the good of the firm.

If you want the people you lead to perform at their peak effectiveness, you must induce them to follow you because they want to, not because they have to. Your people should believe in what they are doing, and see how the work you ask them to do can help them achieve their ambitions. To turn a team into a high-performing coalition, its leader needs to understand what drives each member. As David Guo, CEO of Display Research Laboratories, says: 'The goal of the leader is to understand what motivates people and leverage that, not just show them a path.'

People yearn to become the best they can be. If they don't believe in their leaders, in the organization's strategy or in the approaches they are asked to take, they will not follow with enthusiasm. The authors have coached many managers who are biding their time, hoping their incompetent bosses will be 'found out' and move on. Very few of us are willing to do our best for poor leaders or incompetent managers.

Long-term relationships can never be mutually beneficial unless agendas are dovetailed. Irrespective of whether people are above, below or equal to you in the organization's hierarchy, they will only help you get what you want if you help them get what they want, and they will not adopt your goals unless they have reason to believe that, in doing so, they will further their own. The secret, therefore, is to create a partnership based on mutual self-interest.

The first step when aligning the agendas of your followers with the agenda of the organization, is to align your own business and personal agendas, as described in Chapter 4. What you do, and the conviction with which you do it, set the standards for others. If your own business and personal agendas are obviously in alignment, your followers will see the value of making the compromises their alignment requires. If you yourself have a business agenda that meets your personal goals, you will be motivated to achieve your business goals. If you are advancing your personal goals that are in support of your business goals, you are using the organization in a congruent way. High performance results when you align or dovetail both agendas in yourself, so that your actions fulfil both sets of objectives.

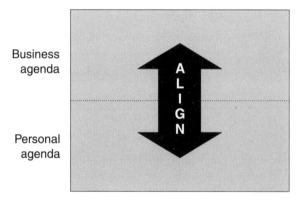

Figure 5.1   *Personal alignment*

Once you have aligned your own agendas, the next step is to understand what other people want. You will have a clear idea about the business agendas of people who work for you, and may even have set them yourself, but their personal agendas will be more or less obscure. It is not enough to imagine what you would want, if you were them. If you are to earn their loyalty, by helping them to achieve something important to them, you will know them and what they value at a much deeper level than that.

Logic and reason play their parts in how we see our world and judge what is or is not in our interests, but we are social animals deeply concerned with non-rational qualities such as our reputations, self-esteem, status and the

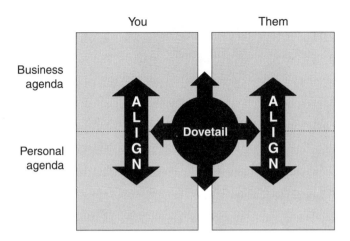

Figure 5.2 *Dovetailing agendas*

positions we hold in the various hierarchies we find ourselves in. Does the following anecdote ring any bells?

The reengineering programme of a European healthcare provider was being blocked by an influential senior researcher who did not understand the reasons for the proposed changes, but spoke eloquently against them at every opportunity. A careful assessment of his personal and clinical objectives revealed that his real concern was that the reengineering programme would prevent the funding of a new professorship vital to his research projects. Since it was likely that the reengineering programme would fail to deliver the projected benefits for patients if he continued to oppose it, it was an easy decision to use some of the programme's budget to fund the new chair. In this way, the aims of the institution (clinical and process excellence) and the aims of the researcher (clinical excellence and personal status) were reconciled.

The higher up the management hierarchy you climb, the more time you need to spend on managing relationships, because the issues tend to become fuzzier and your relationships with your 'stakeholders' tend to become more complex. By 'stakeholders' we mean anyone who has a 'stake' – something to win or lose – from the success or failure of your activities.

The four categories of stakeholder are as follows:

1. *Upward stakeholders.* These are your boss and the other key people at this level in the organization who have influence over your activities

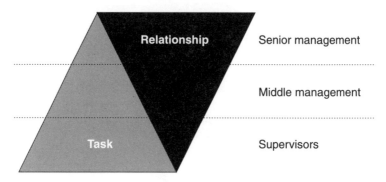

Figure 5.3 *Task and relationship*

and can either support or sabotage your initiatives depending on how well you manage them. You may also need to manage your boss' boss and his or her peer group. The more you satisfy the needs of senior managers, the more influence you will have in the areas that matter to you.

2. *Your peers.* Maintaining good relations with your peers is vital for a number of reasons: they may share your objectives; you may be dependent on them for the success of your initiatives; their views of you will affect how you are perceived by the people they influence; their views may be canvassed by senior managers when you are being considered for promotion.

3. *Your direct reports and other staff.* Your ability to help your bosses meet their goals will depend on your skill at delegating the mundane, day-to-day stuff that comes across your desk. We will look at the art of delegation in more detail in Chapter 7. For now, we will just note that the more effective a 'coach' you are for those who work for you, the more they will be able to manage themselves, and the more time you will have to deliver value to your upward stakeholders.

4. *External stakeholders.* Customers, suppliers, investors, neighbours, the media, etc. As the Dilts Strategy Group's research into Silicon Valley growth companies shows, who you know and the quality of your networks is as important for the valuation of your company as your technology.

The number of stakeholders you have to create 'wins' for, and the number of agendas you have to understand and monitor, mean you have to devote a great deal of time to relationship management and alignment.

Much of the capacity liberated by the prioritization and delegation skills we discuss in Chapter 7 can be most usefully applied to these activities.

Positive intention

A young mother, Myriam, was busy upstairs with the vacuum cleaner. She had left her three-year-old daughter with a drink, watching a *Toy Story* video, and everything was quiet. Suddenly, there was a huge crash. Myriam rushed downstairs into the kitchen and found water and broken dishes all over the floor. Her instinctive reaction was to go ballistic, and send her daughter out of the room while she cleaned up the mess. She suppressed the urge and instead asked calmly: 'What were you trying to do?'

'Sorry mummy, I was trying to help you with the washing up,' was the shocked and tearful reply.

Myriam's restraint, and her interest in motive rather than outcome, gave her more options. 'Thanks, but let me show you a different way to wash up,' she said, 'and this time, let's use plastic dishes.' By looking for a 'positive intention', Myriam turned a disaster into a lesson, and rewarded the worthy motive, instead of punishing the messy outcome.

An ability to identify positive intention is vital when you're dovetailing agendas, but it is easier said than done. It is not easy when you feel the organization is run by a bunch of half-wits with an inflated sense of their own importance who do not seem to understand the basics of your department. It is even worse if those half-wits are on secondment or short-term assignments, and you will have to live with the decisions they make today, after they move on.

Blaming others for the failure or inadequacies of your part of the business or project may relieve your emotional tension for a while, and may even be justified, but it does not help. As Giles Pageot, CEO of Pharmacia, said: 'I have no illusions about human nature, so I don't have any negative surprises, but I also have a strong belief about what's possible.'

When individuals object to a reengineering programme or to some other change in their circumstances, you must try to understand their positive intention and take responsibility for changing their opinion. Try to separate in your mind unhelpful or unproductive behaviour from what motivates it. You may be able to empathize with their intention and find ways to give them what they need without abandoning your plans.

All behaviour has a positive intention and provides some apparent benefit to the person concerned. The choice of behaviour may be limited, or stem from a psychological inflexibility, but it always serves a purpose. We all choose what appears to us to be the best choice available, at the time. If you can get yourself into the habit of looking for the positive intentions, you can break through negative feelings and attitudes, and get stalled projects and programmes moving again. As Monty Roberts, the horse whisperer, put it: 'Hold in your mind the idea that the horse can do no wrong; that whatever action he takes was most likely influenced by you.'[8] That is a good idea to hold in your mind when you are dealing with people, too.

We do not mean by this that all behaviour is positively motivated. People may act with cynicism, or with malice, but they will always act in the belief that their behaviour will achieve something for them. If you act *as if* there is a positive intention, and seek to understand what they want to achieve, you will be better able to influence them.

Strategies for matching: the structure of influence

Differences in personality, communication, thinking style, values and culture can sometimes derail communication, even when both parties seek similar objectives. It is not enough to want to cooperate – we need the competency to present our ideas and to negotiate any blockers or pitfalls that we encounter along the way.

Milton Erickson, one of the fathers of modern psychotherapy, told the story of his young son, nearly hysterical after a bad fall and a deep cut on his knee. The child's panic was making it very difficult to treat him. Expressions of alarm and concern would have added to the boy's anxiety, so Erickson talked about the boy's immediate concerns and focus of attention – the redness of the blood, the number of stitches the wound would need and how long it would take to heal. Once the boy was a little calmer, Erickson moved him on: he talked about how much better his scar would be than his brother's, and how proud he could be of it. Only then did he start to administer the necessary treatment.

This approach to relationship management is known as 'match, pace, lead'. Erickson 'matched' the boy by talking to him about what he was experiencing in the moment; 'paced' him (shifted his focus) by playing on his fraternal rivalry; and 'led' him to the desired outcome.

When people are naturally and spontaneously in rapport with each other, they start to match each other on a fundamental physiological level: their body postures will become similar; they will start to speak at the same speed and volume of voice; they will pick up on each other's key words; and they will naturally use each other's language. If you want proof of this, watch romantic couples or close friends eating together in a restaurant, or observe non-verbal behaviours in meetings. Observe the similarity in body posture between those who are aligned or in rapport, and those who are not.

When Roger Welsh, chairman of a project management software company, went to a meeting to discuss a price for the sale of his company to an aerospace engineering firm, he opened discussions by reminding the negotiating team of what had happened so far:

> We first met on 13th of September and you [*nodding at a member of the other company's team*] and George attended that meeting. We then visited our development office in Windsor and our North American branch offices and, in December, some of your technical people reviewed our product, benchmarked it against our competitors' products. They reported back to you saying that we had a significant competitive advantage over our competitors [*people in the room nodded their heads in agreement*], you did due diligence and John and I came to your headquarters in Detroit to meet the Board and answer questions about the company [*more nods*]. More recently, some of your senior sales and marketing people have visited our sales offices in the US, Europe and Asia. In the light of your evaluation and investigations of our company, products and marketplace, I am sure you will agree that $120 million is a reasonable price for the company.

After a brief negotiation, a price of $110 million was agreed – at least $10 million more than Welsh's company had been hoping for, but still considered a good deal by the acquirer.

Welsh was using a classic influence strategy. He told the other negotiating team a long list of things they knew to be true, and followed this with a statement that was open to debate: '. . . You will agree that a price of $120m is reasonable.' Because the other side agreed with the initial statements they were inclined to feel comfortable with the final statement.

If someone tells you things you know to be true, or that you discover later to be true, you will become increasingly likely to believe (trust) what he or she says next. In other words, if you 'match' something they already know to get in step with them, you can then lead them somewhere else.

This technique is very powerful, and is open to abuse because it gives you a degree of cognitive control over your ability to build trust with people.

This is why we opened this chapter with an emphasis on dovetailing agendas, because Alpha leaders only use these powerful influence tools in support of success for *all* parties. Short-term wins over your colleagues, customers, or suppliers do not build long-term relationships of trust.

Matching, pacing and leading can also be useful in emotionally charged situations. After a recent merger of two pharmaceutical companies, a large number of redundancies was announced. Morale among the people who were left was at a low ebb (so-called 'survivor sickness'), and it was proving hard to get the merged organization aligned. Communication representatives were appointed in all departments and trained to match the sadness and anger of the survivors who had lost so many friends and colleagues. They listened to the staff, acknowledged their feelings of dismay, but made no attempt to judge or change them. When people are worried, angry and frustrated, it is quite disarming to feel that, at last, someone has listened and understood your feelings. After 15 or 20 minutes, the emotional intensity would fall and the communication rep could lead the person on to more positive ground, by asking such questions as, 'What can you do to improve the situation? Who can you talk to? What opportunities do you have in the new organization? How can you influence decisions?'

Ideas and words are important for matching, but matching also occurs in the non-verbal realm. We like and tend to trust people who behave similarly to us, and we are less disposed to trust those who behave differently. The more similar a person is, the more open we are to their influence.

Tools for thought

1. Dovetailing agendas: self, other and observer

One of your challenges is to tap the discretionary energy of those you are leading by helping them dovetail their personal agendas with the business agenda. Leaders skilled in team alignment try to ensure that everyone they work with achieves his or her personal objectives in a way that is consistent with the objectives of the business.

The first step in meeting this challenge is to acquire a deep understanding of the needs, aspirations and motivations of people you wish to influence, because you can only help them to achieve what they want in their lives and their careers if you know what makes them tick.

In traditional Native American culture, all teenagers learn to track animals. It is part of their transition to adulthood. They spend weeks studying the habits of the animals: what they eat, where they sleep, where they go at different times of day and, over longer periods of time, where and when they migrate. The youngsters learn that there are three levels of tracking. The first is when you can see the animal you are following. The second is when you track its footprints and the broken twigs and branches that mark its passage. The third level of tracking is when you connect your soul to the animal's soul.

Managing your key relationships can be very similar and calls for similar levels of skill. It is worth spending a lot of time getting to know people, and thinking about how you can help them to be more successful.

Take a key relationship (someone at work who is important to you) and study him or her in the following way:

(a) Gather information

Consider everything you know about this person. How old is he? Does he have a partner, and if so, do they have children, and how old are they? How do you think he is doing in his career? What are his aims? What does he believe in and feel strongly about? What are his special talents and skills? What are his interests outside work and family?

The easiest way to gather more information about a person is to have lunch or a drink with him, after work or at the end of the week. It's surprising how much people will tell you about themselves, if you seem interested and willing to listen. Be open about your objective. Say: 'I want to understand you, and what you want from life and your career, so that we can find ways in which we can help each other.'

If such a tête-à-tête is impractical or unsuitable, find other sources of information. Talk to people in his department and others who know him well. If you are going to be presenting to him or seeking his support on behalf of your department or division, it is quite legitimate to call up someone on his team, and say: 'I am presenting some ideas to Joe in a few weeks, and I want to find out what's important to him in this area.' You can then use follow-up questions to get more personal information. There is nothing underhanded or devious about this. You just want to understand him well enough to be able to help him achieve his goals while he helps you achieve yours.

(b) Use your intuition

Once you have sufficient information, 'step into his shoes, with the laces undone'. Imagine you are sitting at his desk and seeing the world and the people entering and leaving his office as he sees them. Imagine you are running his department and dealing with the people he deals with. Think about his 'life balance'. When does he arrive at the office in the morning and leave at night, and what does this imply about his home life and family relationships? Imagine what he does when he gets home. Look at the world from his point of view. What are his hopes and fears?

Think about his personal style. How does he like to receive information – written, spoken, with images, or by seeing for himself? Does he think 'big picture' or 'detail'? Does he see the cup half full or half empty?

(c) Step back into your own shoes

What are your goals and objectives? Which of them require his support or consent? What should be your immediate objectives in your relationship with him?

(d) Take the observer position

Imagine you and he are talking together, and that you are watching from a position where you can see him and that other person who 'looks just like you'. See how these two people are interacting and relating. Try to get a feel for their respective agendas, and imagine how they can be dovetailed, so that the two people can become members of the same team.

If it is not immediately obvious how their agendas can be 'aligned', try chunking up, down and sideways, as explained in Chapter 2.

Think about how both of you can be successful at the same time. Think of the 'quick wins' you can get for him and, if none spring readily to your mind, think of areas where they might be found. A relationship is like a bank account. If you put value in, you get value back later. People remember acts of kindness and assistance, and look for opportunities to reciprocate.

2. Seeking positive intention

To identify positive intention, ask yourself: 'What is this person trying to achieve (by this behaviour) that is so important?' If the answer you come up with is still negative, repeat the question again in the style of chunking up (Chapter 2). For example, Joe is always getting in the way and blocking you. Chunking up may eventually reveal a more positive motive, as we see in Figure 5.4. Once you think you have a good idea about what makes Joe behave the way he does in this situation, you can try out your hypothesis by giving him what he really wants. If you take time to build more rapport with him, he may become more considerate and attentive to feedback.

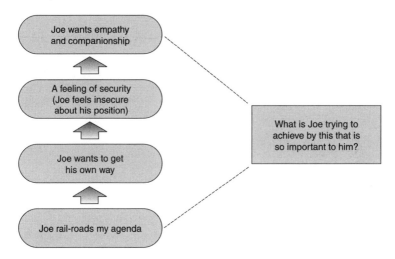

Figure 5.4 *Seeking positive intention*

Use the following two-step process to practise revealing positive intention in the context of difficult working relationships:

1.   Think of someone with whom you work and with whom you would like to have a good relationship, but who displays behaviour that you find difficult. Your judgements about his or her behaviour interfere with your ability to build a good relationship. Ask yourself: 'What is he or she trying to achieve by this behaviour that is so important to him or her?' Take the answer and apply the question to it again, and keep applying the question to the answer until you get an answer that you can empathize with.

     Once you can empathize with the motive for someone's behaviour, you have in fact changed your feeling towards that person. Then you are likely to treat him or her differently, and you may get a positive response.

2. See if you can test your hypothesis about the positive intention: behave towards the individual in a way that meets the need expressed by the positive intention and notice the response. Does the person like it? Does the behaviour towards you change? Does the disruptive behaviour change?

3. Matching communications: thinking style gap analysis

One of the easiest ways we can lose influence with another person is by the simple fact that we think (process information) differently than the person we are trying to influence. By modifying our own style, we can increase our ability to build relationships of trust and influence.

Much has been written about the various thinking styles we use, which are also known as 'metaprogrammes'.[9] In Table 5.1 we give a summary of a few key styles that impact us in business.

Table 5.1   *Key thinking styles*

Thinking style category	Dimensions	
Approach to goals	*Towards the goal* They like to think about the goal and how to get there	*Away from the problem* They like to think about the problem and how to avoid it
Chunk size	*Large chunks* They think in terms of the big picture	*Small chunks* Their thinking tends to be detail orientated
Locus of control	*Proactive* They make the world fit how they think it should be – they are 'self-referenced'	*Reactive* They fit themselves and their projects to the way the world thinks they should be. They are 'other-referenced'
Approach to tasks	*Options and choices* They look for the best way of doing things and like to have options	*Following procedures* They like to follow the tried and tested way of doing things
Point of view	*Self – other people – observer* They look at things from their own point of view (self), from other people's point of view, or as an observer	
Information sorting	*People – Task – Information – Things* They sort information in terms of the impact on people, the delivery of the task, the quality of the information or in terms of the material objects	

If you are about to have an important interaction with someone, take some time to go through the following questions:

1. Assess yourself in terms of these thinking styles. What are your dominant styles?
2. Assess your key stakeholder. What are his or her dominant styles?
3. Look at any mismatches.
4. Plan how you will present information in the areas where your styles mismatch. If necessary, get some input from someone who has a similar thinking style to them.

Use Table 5.2 to help think through your strategies for matching.

Table 5.2 *Matching strategies*

Approach to goals	If they are towards the goal, focus on the vision and the benefits of the vision; if they are away from the problem, talk about how you can help resolve all the issues.
Chunk size	If you are detail oriented and they are big picture, produce a slide set and then *only present the summary* slide. Take the rest of the slides with you to the meeting as back-up in case they ask. If they are detail oriented and you are big picture, spend a significant amount of time working up the details and making sure that you are able to answer their questions. If necessary, use a detail-oriented member of your team to provide the detailed material. Your credibility will depend on it.
Locus of control	Are they going to create the future despite other factors in the world (proactive) or are they going to respond to the influences on them? Present benefits to them in the style in which they think.
Approach to tasks	Do they like to have lots of options, and are they always thinking about the best way of doing things, or do they like to follow tried and tested procedures? Match their preference.
Point of view	Do they think about how your point of view fits their own internal values, logic and criteria; that of key relationships such their own managers or staff; or do they look at it from a broader company point of view?
Sorts information	Deliver information in the way they think. If they think people, present this way. If they are only concerned with action or task, match. If they are interested in information, research, etc., give them that. If they want to talk about physical kit, boxes or houses, match their interest.

4. Planning stakeholder relationships

Each of the three tools described above can be employed in developing an integrated stakeholder management plan. Create a pro forma planning sheet as shown in Figure 5.5, and populate it by answering the following questions:

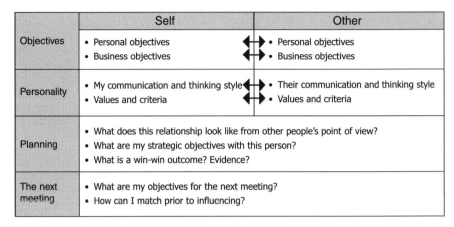

	Self	Other
Objectives	• Personal objectives • Business objectives	• Personal objectives • Business objectives
Personality	• My communication and thinking style • Values and criteria	• Their communication and thinking style • Values and criteria
Planning	• What does this relationship look like from other people's point of view? • What are my strategic objectives with this person? • What is a win-win outcome? Evidence?	
The next meeting	• What are my objectives for the next meeting? • How can I match prior to influencing?	

Figure 5.5 *Planning stakeholder relationships*

1. What are my personal objectives at work?
2. What are my business objectives?
3. What is my objective with this stakeholder?
   - from a personal point of view?
   - from a business point of view?
4. Stepping into the other person's shoes and looking at the world from their point of view:
   - What are their personal objectives at work?
   - What are their business objectives?
5. Compare the communication and thinking styles and values of
   - Yourself;
   - The other person.
   - Search for any places where your communication and thinking style or values are different to theirs (i.e. mismatch).
   - Plan how you can be flexible in your style so as to match them.
6. Stand back and look at yourself in relationship to the other person and ask:
   - How does this relationship look to others?
   - How does it look from the point of view of the team?
   - How does it look from the point of view of the organization?
7. What are my strategic objectives with this person? Where do I want to be in 1 year/6 months/3 months/1 month?
8. How do I dovetail our objectives to achieve a win-win outcome? How will I know that I am being successful at this?

9.   What are my objectives for the next meeting?
   - How will I know that I am being successful?
   - What are the signals (verbal and non-verbal) during the meeting that will act as milestones towards a successful conclusion? What will they look like and sound like?

10.   How can I match them prior to influencing?

For more resources on task through relationship, see
www.AlphaLeaders.com

Conclusion

Relationships are key. If you take care of the relationships, the tasks will take care of themselves. The leader's primary focus should be managing relationships with stakeholders to maximize positive outcomes.

In the next chapter we will look at how you can achieve greater alignment in the culture of the whole organization and create a 'culture that can act'.

References

1.   Mandela, N. (1994) *Long Walk to Freedom*, Little, Brown and Company.
2.   Sampson, A. (1999) *Mandela: The Authorized Biography*, Harper Collins.
3.   De Klerk, F.W. (1999) *The Last Trek: A New Beginning*, Macmillan.
4.   Sampson, A. (1999) *Op. cit.*
5.   De Klerk, F.W. (1999) *Op. cit.*
6.   Axelrod, R. (1990) *The Evolution of Co-operation*, Penguin.
7.   Luciano, R. and Fisher, D. (1982) *The Umpire Strikes Back*, Bantam Books.
8.   Roberts, M. (1996) *The Man Who Listens to Horses*, Hutchinson.
9.   Metaprogrammes were developed by Leslie Cameron Bandler and others, and written about in a variety of works including Charvet, S.R. (1997) *Words that Change Minds, Mastering the Language of Influence*, Kendall/Hunt.

6

Creating Cultures That Can Act

*There's no limit to what a man can do so long as he does not
care a straw who gets the credit for it*
Charles Edward Montague

The Minnesota Mining and Manufacturing Company (3M) was founded in
1902. It struggled in its early years, like most new businesses, before assuring its future in 1914 with the launch of an abrasive cloth, called 'Three-M-
ite', made with aluminum oxide. It was much better than natural mineral
emery for cutting metal, and was used in huge quantities in the First World
War. The company paid its first dividend in 1916 and has not missed a
quarterly cash payment to shareholders since.[1]

William L. McKnight joined the firm as an assistant bookkeeper in 1907
and rose through the ranks, becoming president in 1929 and chairman in
1949. He is still revered as the firm's great 'philosopher-leader' and the principal architect of 3M's famously innovative corporate culture, a culture that
has been described by management writers Christopher Bartlett and
Sumantra Ghoshal as 'an organizational climate that stimulates ordinary
people to produce extraordinary performance'.[2]

There are many examples of the innovations nurtured by 3M's tolerance
of non-conformity and appreciation of genius. The story of one such invention begins in 1922, when 3M employee Dick Drew paid an afternoon visit
to an autobody shop to test a new batch of sandpaper. 3M's patented
Wetordry sandpaper was at the time the standard product in auto paint and
repair shops because of its smooth finish and reduced dust hazard.

Drew heard a group of workers cursing vehemently. Two-tone cars had
recently become popular, but painters hated them because they had to mask
parts of the autobody with heavy adhesive tape and butcher paper, and

when they later removed the masking, some of the new paint often came away with it. As he watched the craftsmen repair the torn paint, Drew might have thought of all that extra Wetordry he could sell them. But instead he thought of a solution to the problem: a tape with a less aggressive adhesive. He also realized 3M was ideally placed to develop such tape, because it would be like sandpaper without the sand.

Drew returned to the laboratory, and began a long and frustrating quest for the right combination of adhesive and backing. After several fruitless years, 3M President McKnight told Drew to drop the project and get back to work on improving sandpaper. Drew duly complied, but a day later he thought of a new way to handle the backing problems and resumed his experiments. In the middle of one of them, McKnight paid another visit to the lab, saw Drew hard at work on his supposedly abandoned project, but said nothing.

Drew finally found the right combination of materials and asked McKnight to approve funding for a paper-making machine to manufacture the new tape. His request was rejected, but Drew wasn't about to give up now. As a researcher, he had authority to approve purchases of up to $100, so he began writing a series of $99 purchase orders. He later confessed his strategy to McKnight while showing him the new machine.

And in this way, masking tape was born. Its launch marked the start of a new chapter in 3M's evolution, which would lead to the launch of Scotch Cellophane tape (also invented by Drew) in 1930, and to 3M's current range of over 700 tapes for medical, electrical, construction and dozens of other applications.

These exchanges between McKnight and Drew, Drew's insubordinate purchase of the paper-making machinery and McKnight's relaxed response to his defiance, are among the most hallowed in 3M's annals. 'They set forth a clear ethic for managers,' the company states in its literature. 'If you have the right person on the right project, and they are absolutely dedicated to finding a solution, leave them alone. Tolerate their initiative and trust them.'

Stories such as these play an important role in creating and refreshing the 3M culture. The company says they 'help us [understand] the many sources of our innovative culture; and the importance of our . . . desire to challenge and encourage each other, as we look for . . . new ways to meet customer needs and solve customer problems.'

McKnight's Management Principles, which he articulated in 1948, give further insight into the organizational framework within which 3M's innovations flourish:

> As our business grows, it becomes increasingly necessary to delegate responsibility and to encourage men and women to exercise their initiative. This requires considerable tolerance. Those men and women to whom we delegate authority and responsibility, if they are good people, are going to want to do their jobs in their own way.
>
> Mistakes will be made. But if a person is essentially right, the mistakes he or she makes are not as serious in the long run as the mistakes management will make if it undertakes to tell those in authority exactly how they must do their jobs.
>
> Management that is destructively critical when mistakes are made kills initiative. And it's essential that we have many people with initiative if we are to continue to grow.[3]

McKnight did not invent anything but, through the way he managed people, he helped to create and maintain an atmosphere at 3M that favoured invention. Leaders make things happen by forming coalitions of people intent on action. These coalitions are often so fluid it may be hard to say who formed or led them, but it does not really matter who gets the credit. Good leadership is more evident in its consequences than its execution. The job of leaders is to liberate the potential of those who report to them, creating cultures that can act in accordance with the goals of the company.

In short their job is to get the job done, not by doing it, but by ensuring the right people are assembled together, in the right circumstances, at the right time, with adequate resources. In Chapter 5 we argued that if you look after the relationships, the tasks will look after themselves. Here we extend this further and say that if you look after the organizational culture – the values that are acted out in the web of relationships between all the members of the organization – then the members of the firm will self-organize in a way best suited to achieving shared business objectives.

The 3M story suggests that three powerful drivers are available to you when developing an organization that can act. The first is a coherent culture, aligned in all important dimensions, so that what people believe is matched to their competencies and their behaviours. Because innovation is vital at 3M, the company's values and practices are designed to maintain a climate conducive to innovation.

The second driver is a licence for non-conformists, such as Drew, to act as they see fit, unimpeded by rules and regulations.

The third driver is a set of mechanisms and rules that embody the spirit of the company and bypass bureaucracy. In 1956 3M introduced just such a mechanism with its now world-famous policy of urging scientists to spend 15% of their time experimenting in areas of their own choice.

Creating coherent cultures

Imagine your most recent flight. You are settling into your seat, relaxing with some reading, perhaps reviewing your e-mails. The pilot comes over the public address system welcoming you on board, but then announces that you are all now going to fly this plane yourselves – all 300 passengers working together simultaneously. A worrying announcement certainly, and one that is likely to have you thinking that you have a pretty low probability of success.

This is exactly the experience that San Francisco company, Cinematrix, simulates for large corporate audiences.[4] A computer flight simulation allows large groups of people to pilot a simulated plane with indicators whose movements are picked up by video cameras, and then processed into commands to the computerized aircraft's controls. The group works together to steer the plane through the targets they see on a large screen at the front of the room.

The instructions are simple enough: those on the left of the room make the plane go left and right by moving their indicators left and right. Those on the right of the room make the plane go up and down by moving their indicators forward and back. The video cameras recording the movements of the indicators take an average of what they see and instruct the simulated aircraft accordingly. But how do all 300 people move those indicators just the right amounts to steer the aircraft precisely? It seems impossible; there are too many variables – 300 different reaction times, 300 different levels of hand–eye coordination skill.

In a typical simulation, initial scepticism seems justified. The virtual plane careers all over the sky, narrowly missing mountains one second, and valley bottoms the next. But in a little while, the group 'catches' it. Order emerges from chaotic movement. The group adjusts to the complexities of the collective task, and before long people are whooping triumphantly as the plane smashes through one target after another. The group aligns itself.

Each person remains a unique individual, but at that time, in that place, in pursuit of a common task, they become one.

The computer simulation of collective piloting is a lot of fun, but it reveals in a thrilling way, that makes the hairs stand up on the back of your neck, something profoundly important about human nature. It shows that in certain circumstances individuals can take great pleasure in acting successfully in concert. Given a sufficiently clear and meaningful task, and strong alignment within the group, we actually enjoy surrendering our selves in the pursuit of a common goal.

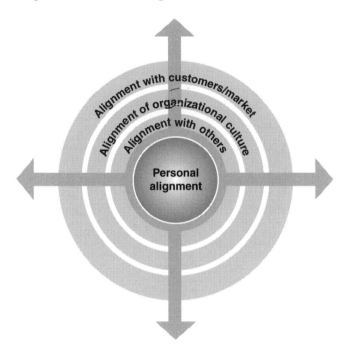

Figure 6.1   *Coherent cultures*

Organizations are more than the sum of their members. There are 'synergies' (habits, conventions, routines, attitudes, blind spots and ways of doing things) that live in the walls and floors of the organization. Creating a climate in which everyone can work at a high degree of effectiveness is easier said than done and requires a high degree of organizational alignment on all the logical levels we described in Chapter 4. There we talked about personal alignment. Here we are not only talking about the alignment of the entire organization within the organizational 'skin', but also its alignment with customers and marketplace.

Just as we can increase our level of personal alignment on each of the six levels, so too can the organization align more effectively across a wide spectrum of experience. Each movement up the pyramid brings more of the whole system into view, and each requires different types of leadership processes and interactions that incorporate and operate on information from the level below it to create a truly coherent culture (Figure 6.1).

Context

No man or organization is an island. We, and the organizations with which we are associated, are all parts of larger systems, such as nations, societies, cultures and professions. Kevin Roberts, CEO of Saatchi & Saatchi, has said that organizational *culture* is a misnomer, and that what we should be talking about is organizational *spirit*. This spirit is best engaged when we connect to the context around us that stretches beyond the bounds of the individual corporation.

We all want to do something useful with our lives, but many of us find it difficult to reconcile what we do to earn a living with our desire to leave a legacy or make a difference. The clearer an organization is about how it makes a difference, the more motivated people will become. For example, a pharmaceutical company doesn't just make drugs; you could say it 'heals the world'. People working in pharmaceutical companies are often more motivated by the social contribution of their work than by the share price, but few companies leverage this. A company can motivate people who are income oriented by bonus schemes and share schemes, and this is entirely compatible with motivating people by providing social value. If you can't pay everyone a lot, you had better get them excited about what you are doing!

Global players are recognizing increasingly that the social impact of their work affects customer perception of the company and consequently has an impact on sales. Even companies in the mainstream can make progress in this direction. Barclays Bank is making a concerted effort to make it easier for customers to interact with them. For example, CEO Matt Barrett and equal opportunities and diversity director Niccola Swann have recognized that by putting significant additional resources into their diversity programme, they will benefit their own staff, become more appealing to

Britain's increasingly important ethnic minority population and other diverse groups, and make a contribution to British culture in general.

Identity

When Kevin Roberts took over as CEO of Saatchi & Saatchi, he inherited a failing company with flagging sales. In a relatively short space of time, with revenues up 10% and record new billings in 1999, he sold Saatchi & Saatchi to Publicis for $2 billion – not a bad achievement for his first few years with the company.

Roberts says: 'I didn't bring in any new people. I did it with the team that was there.' He established a profound identity for the firm that people could engage with at all levels, calling Saatchi 'the hottest ideas shop on the planet'. Added to the firm credo 'nothing is impossible', Roberts was able to lift the performance of the organization as a whole, building a sense of community, belonging and contributing.[5]

An organization's identity has two facets:

- Our purpose, role or mission: What is the special contribution we make to our customers and the market?
- Our vision: What are we aiming for in the future? What do we want to make happen?

Purpose

Organizational alignment at an identity level will be easier to achieve where an organization's purpose is defined in terms of the value added to the customer. For example, Storage Tek, the global information storage provider, sells enormous hard drives the size of rooms in which companies store their electronic information. Until recently they thought of themselves as selling 'storage boxes'. They have now looked at the value they offer to their customers, and say that their mission is 'to expand the world's access to information and knowledge', with the slogan 'information made powerful'.

This shift has radically changed the way they think about what it is that they are selling, and gives greater scope for employees to connect to the company's purpose – it is a lot easier to get excited about 'information made powerful' than 'storage boxes'.

Vision

Vision is another important component of identity, and is an expression of where you want to be. It is what Jim Collins and Jerry Porras[6] call a BHAG – a Big Hairy Audacious Goal that fulfils your mission.

Ted Turner's vision for CNN was to be 'the world's news leader', and it is. A couple of decades ago this would have seemed audacious, but CNN is now an accepted global institution.

The vision needs to be based on the organization's purpose, because its purpose reflects the value created by the products and services of the organization, and the vision needs to be grounded in its competencies. The vision needs to be both highly ambitious and realistic. It also needs to appeal to everyone in the organization, as it can be key to getting the organization aligned.

It is worth noting that the identity of the organization is not something that can be dreamed up by marketing consultants or branding agencies. In just the same way as a healthy person's identity emerges naturally rather than being artificially constructed, the same happens for companies. The closer your purpose statement and your vision are to the 'soul' of the organization, the easier it will be for the organization to align behind it.

Values and beliefs

Customers are increasingly discriminating in their acceptance of marketing campaigns, and increasingly aware of divergence between espoused brand values and the values of the organization itself. Alignment of values promotes congruence – and recognizes inconsistencies – within and beyond the organization.

As Jasper Kunde says:

> Strong brand positions are about having confidence in your own powers. And in the belief that what your company does is right . . . To be able to work with the qualitative values of brands, the company must manage via a set of attitudes and values . . . Only when these attitudes and values go hand in hand with skills – the whole thing being managed using a Corporate Religion – will the company be equipped to attain the ultimate position of a brand religion.[7]

We may find the phrase 'corporate religion' a little frightening and it may remind us of religious fundamentalism, but one only has to think of Disney, Harley Davidson, Coca-Cola, Microsoft, Apple, Starbuck's, McDonald's,

CNN and Hard Rock Café to understand that converging the company culture with the brand values is very powerful indeed.

Kevin Roberts goes one step further, and maintains that 'brands are dead. Customers are looking for love marks – customers want a relationship . . . We need to build an emotional lifeline between consumers' hearts and producers' brands'.[8] He points out that products like the iMac, or the VW Beetle, inspire a level of affection and association in people that goes far beyond other computers or cars. To achieve this degree of connectedness requires powerful internal value alignment.

Our values are the principles that help guide our behaviour. Our values reflect the core of our identity, and are the lens through which we execute our goals. Values unite a company around its purpose and vision. We need to ask the question, what is important to us as a team, and as part of the larger organization, as we move towards accomplishing our vision and strategic goals? The congruence of our stated values and our actual practices is pivotal to the organization's success.

The most common way leaders try to influence attitudes and beliefs in their organization is through major set piece presentations and through the use of motivational speakers. These speakers and presentations address a whole range of issues:

- Be the best you can be.
- Continuously improve.
- Quality is everything.
- People matter most.
- The organization is in constant change – all you have is your skills and your competencies, develop yourself.
- The customer is always right.
- Each member of staff should take personal accountability for the success of the firm.

However, internal conferences and one-day events often have a bad reputation among managers and staff because the intervention is usually too small to produce any change in the organization. People get cynical about taking time away from their busy desks to hear the CEO or divisional director promote the latest management fad, which quickly fades away as the organization gradually reverts to the old way of doing things.

Like any entity, organizations seek equilibrium, and beliefs will not change unless there is a significant effort to help them change, to reinforce the change, and to measure it. There are four main types of intervention that can help changes in belief:

1. *Restating and elaborating the desired belief with examples, stories and management behaviour.* This is the simplest and most direct way of changing beliefs and values, but it requires tenacity and dogged persistence. It can take years of continuous reinforcement, and a range of methods should be used. These could include internal communication and presentations to promote the ethos and the heroes and heroines of the new culture; recognition systems such as 'awards', and an overhaul of company procedures to ensure that they are consistent with the new values, among other things.

    Ultimately, the most effective way of ensuring that management and staff implement company values is by describing the competencies and behaviours that support the values, and tying those behaviours to annual assessment and compensation schemes. However, many organizations do not have a culture of effective management coaching, assessment and development. One of our coaching clients works for an international company that requires managers to give their staff feedback annually. His boss handed him half a sheet of paper with some hand-written bullet points as he left the room at the end of a meeting saying 'here's your annual assessment'. The first step may therefore be to train managers to use assessment and feedback techniques effectively.

2. *Discrediting the existing belief over time.* The only way the organization will know that management are serious about discrediting the old ways of doing things is to retire or move sideways leaders who expound or champion the old values. Sometimes a board thinks it can keep 'the dinosaur' on the board while changing the culture in the rest of the organization. This doesn't work. If the CEO can't demonstrate his or her commitment to the change programme by making hard decisions, then the change programme is a waste of time.

3. *Changes in capability.* If you reinforce a new skill through training and on-the-job support, new beliefs may emerge. Investment in communications skills development, in particular, will impact values, since

communication is so strongly intertwined with people's sense of values. Again, measurement and assessment of these competencies will increase their importance in the eyes of staff and managers and consequently accelerate their speed of development.

4. *Changes in identity.* If you change the organization's or department's mission and the definition of people's roles, this can change the values they bring to the situation. For example, if you stop saying 'We are IT people', and start saying 'We are business people who design and run the business systems', the beliefs you have about the value of technological solutions can change from 'It's the state of the art' to 'It provides/does not provide cost savings or competitive advantage'.

Capabilities and competencies

Demetrius Comino founded the DEXION Group, which was responsible for developing the Dexion Slotted Angle used in industrial storage shelving throughout the world. He had selected a group of young managers he wanted to develop, and he ran discussion groups at lunchtime in his office to build their leadership capabilities. He covered a vast array of topics and, during a difficult period for the company, ran discussions on evolution and the principles of adaptation to the environment.

One of the managers present at these sessions criticized the approach, saying, 'There's a storm blowing, the ship is heading for the rocks, and the captain is in the cabin giving a talk on evolution.' It would have been easy for Comino to abandon his efforts, to focus on the short-term issues instead of long-term leadership development. But he didn't, and from this group came the senior management who successfully grew the company over the next 20 years. As a result of Comino's care and attention to developing their skills, and his sponsorship of them as individuals, the group felt great loyalty to him and to the company. People development became a religion within the company, to be sustained in good times and bad, regardless of economic pressures.

The long-term development of your best people gives competitive advantage. It is worth noting how easy it is to sacrifice the long-term development of the company for short-term profits. In so doing, the coherence of the organization's culture will disintegrate, as short-term pressures take precedence over the development of competencies that support the way the organization delivers value over the long term. It is also worth remembering, when faced with this kind of trade-off, that the long term is, after all, only a series of short terms.

Behaviours

The best way to affect behaviours, and to increase the alignment of values, beliefs, identity and the way the organization operates, is, of course, to 'walk your talk'. If you say you value a learning culture, then spend time on scanning for new ideas, sharing know-how, implementing knowledge management processes and developing the organization's capacity to absorb new information. If you say you value customer intimacy, spend time interacting with customers, tracking and sharing their feedback, and using multidisciplinary teams to make sense of their input and operationalize it.

Former CEO of publishing group Pearson, Marjorie Scardino, showed this alignment of values and behaviour on 11 September 2001. Her first act after the tragedy of the World Trade Center disaster was to e-mail her staff, 'Be guided by what you and your families need right now. There is no meeting you have to go to and no plane you have to get on if you don't feel comfortable doing it. For now, look to yourselves and your families, and to Pearson to help you in any way we can.'[9]

It is essential for leaders to do an informal audit of their own behaviours in relation to the mission, values and competencies they are promoting in the organization. Since we all have blind spots, it is also important to listen carefully to feedback and *never* to discount persistent feedback as 'unimportant'.

To create a culture that is aligned, do an informal or formal audit of processes, procedures and leadership behaviour in relation to the espoused organizational values. If you don't fix any discrepancy you find, you won't get people to change their own behaviour.

Environment

Our external context can have significant influence over the way we act. By designing and reorganizing environmental factors, such as types of space, food, noise level and seating arrangements, leaders can affect the way people work and improve organizational alignment.

A professional services firm provides a simple example of how layout can improve alignment around values and promote congruent behaviours. Secretaries were not very good at covering for each other when one of them was on holiday or off sick, as they identified very closely with their boss rather than with their peers. The firm was working hard to promote teaming and a strong customer service orientation, but the secretarial team was resistant to attempts to change its working practices. Their desks were isolated from one another, located in proximity to their boss's office. The office layout was already open plan, however, and it was relatively easy to seat the secretaries together in clusters of four desks. As a result they interacted more, picked up the phone for each other and, due to their growing personal relationships, started to brief each other to take care of important incoming work when they were away from the office.

Retaining the non-conformists: encouraging rogue monkeys

To be able to act quickly and powerfully, cultures must tap sources of collective energy, but they must also nurture and respect the unconventional, individualistic, 'rogue' behaviour from which originality and creativity often emerge. Acting together successfully is only desirable to a degree. Taken too far, it can trap a culture in habits and conventions that may be very hard to escape from if they become counter-productive.

It is easy, especially in large organizations, to make happen what has always happened. The trick is to encourage people who make what is *needed* happen. These are people who don't conform, who make things happen differently and who challenge the status quo. As we saw with the 3M story, Drew would not have invented masking tape if he had followed his boss's orders, and if McKnight had not turned a blind eye to his activities.

Studies of monkeys have highlighted the danger of too much conformity and the power of the individualist. Half a dozen monkeys were held together in a large cage. A bunch of bananas was hung from the top of a set of stairs. The cage was rigged so that as soon as one of the monkeys started to climb the stairs, all the monkeys in the cage got soaked with a high-pressure jet of cold water. Very quickly the monkeys learnt to avoid the stairs, and to prevent their fellow monkeys from getting too near them.

When one of the monkeys was removed from the cage and replaced with a new one, the newcomer would naturally think that the bananas were there for the taking, and would begin to move towards the stairs. At that point the whole group would leap on the new monkey and keep him away from the stairs and the tempting bananas. Pretty soon the new monkey learnt the rule 'these stairs are off limits', despite not having experienced the cold water itself.

Over time, all the monkeys were removed one by one from the cage, and new monkeys substituted. The group taught each new monkey in turn that 'these stairs are off limits'. The taboo against touching them was perpetuated, even though by the end of the study, none of the monkeys in the cage had experienced first hand the negative reinforcement of the water-jets used on the original group of monkeys. Long after the experimenters turned off the water-jets, the taboo continued because 'that's how it has always been around here'.

The only way to break the pattern is to introduce into the cage a 'rogue' monkey who flouts the convention, climbs the stairs despite the other monkeys' protests, and gets to eat the bananas. After watching in horror for a while, the group members begin to try out the stairs too. After a while, they are all using the stairs to get bananas, and have all benefited from the actions of the single rogue monkey.

Non-conformists can be extremely successful, even in the most conservative business contexts. In the late 1970s, one of IBM's top performing salespeople in the City of London was called Christopher Bowers. Chris became a member of a spiritual movement organized by a popular Indian guru, Bhagwan Shri Rajneesh. He became ordained as a sanyasin, and started going to work in his religious dress. In those days, the IBM dress code was a white shirt, smart tie and blue pin-stripe suit. Christopher started turning up to work in a red suit, pink shirt, and a bead necklace with a picture of his guru on it. Since he was such a successful salesperson, his bosses didn't know what to do, especially as he had such key relationships with big city banks. His customers, however, thought the whole thing very amusing and eccentric, and continued to buy mainframes from him. As Chris's boss explained: 'It is OK to have the occasional wild duck as long as the rest fly in formation.'

Of course, the extent to which you can let 'rogue monkeys' experiment is determined by the degree of risk involved. It has been suggested that the engineers at the Russian nuclear plant at Chernobyl were experimenting with safety procedures before the catastrophic explosion. At a major car company a consistently reinforced total quality programme went one step too far when some of the shopfloor people changed the order in which they put parts on the car without consulting safety engineers and taking into account the wider effects of their changes.

In *Organizations in Action*, J.D. Thompson defines organizational systems against two dimensions: whether they are simple or complex, and whether they are stable or unstable.[10]

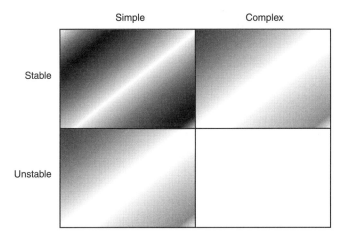

Figure 6.2 *Organizational systems*
Thompson, J.D. (1967) *Organizations in Action*. Reproduced by permission of the McGraw-Hill Companies.

Proactive innovators can be 'let loose' in simple stable systems, and in complex stable systems, where risk assessment is relatively straightforward. Even in simple unstable systems, it may be possible to evaluate risk. However, in complex unstable systems, management needs to keep a firm grip on processes and manage the rogue monkeys carefully.

Saatchi's Kevin Roberts put it in a nutshell when he said: 'I want people who disrupt, but I want them to disrupt *within a team*.'[11]

Bypassing the system: catalytic mechanisms

How can you stop the lethargy and inertia of organizations from stifling the rogue monkeys, the innovators and the entrepreneurs? One answer is to introduce catalytic mechanisms into the business, a term coined by management guru Jim Collins to describe processes that allow members of an organization to by-pass its bureaucracy,[12] and mechanisms that allow organizations greater freedom to act by providing short-cuts through officialdom.

Catalytic mechanisms are the crucial link in aligning an audacious vision to performance. Collins lists five key characteristics of catalytic mechanisms:

1. A catalytic mechanism produces desired results in unpredictable ways. It is not about creating more management controls, but releasing people from the constraints of bureaucracy.
2. A catalytic mechanism distributes power for the benefit of the overall system, often to the great discomfort of those who traditionally hold power. It overrides the vested interests that create inertia.
3. A catalytic mechanism has teeth. A circuit division at Hewlett-Packard didn't wake up until the manufacturing divisions were allowed to buy their components from outside suppliers if they wanted.
4. A catalytic mechanism ejects viruses. It gets too hot for people who are unproductive and they leave of their own accord. Ricardo Semmler, Brazil's famous entrepreneur, would have staff assess their managers and then post the results in public places for all to see. This brutal mechanism soon got rid of ineffective managers.
5. A catalytic mechanism produces an on-going effect. It is not just a one-month wonder, but works over time. In various forms, 3M's 15% rule has operated for more than 40 years.

There is a wide variety of catalytic mechanisms. For example, a US government initiative to eliminate bureaucracy has two simple rules:

1. Waiver-of-regulation requests must be acted upon within 30 days. If there is no answer within 30 days the person requesting the waiver can assume approval and implement the waiver.
2. Those officials who have the power to change regulations can approve a waiver request, but only the head of an agency can deny a request.

The CEO of GE Capital wanted to stimulate original thinking in the divisions of GE Capital, so the annual strategic planning process for each division is conducted as a 'live' workshop for which no pre-planning or presentations are allowed, and which he himself attends personally.

Royal Dutch Shell's GameChanger process was set up to stimulate growth in the Exploration and Production (E&P) division. A small panel of free-thinking employees was given the authority to allocate $20 million to rule-breaking, game-changing ideas submitted by their peers.

- Anyone with an idea can present a 10-minute pitch. The panel gets around 10 submissions a month.
- Approved ideas get a small amount of funding ($100 000–$600 000) within 8–10 days.
- The idea-owner has to attract a team to work on the idea.
- After several months, each project goes through a proof-of-concept review at which point it enters Shell's normal investment allocation process.

Of Shell's five largest growth initiatives in early 1999, four had their genesis in the GameChanger process.

Collins suggests that there are a few general principles that support the process of building effective catalytic mechanisms:

- Don't just add, remove: less can be better. What policies do you need to remove?
- Create, don't copy: dovetail to your precise situation.
- Use money, but not only money: other things motivate human behaviour.
- Allow your mechanisms to evolve: use the principles of in-course correction that we discuss in Chapter 8.
- Build an integrated set. A whole system of reinforcing initiatives works better than a single one.

Tools for thought

1. Aligning organizational culture: culture gap analysis

Whether one is carrying out an ambitious exercise to integrate brand values and internal organizational values, or simply helping the organization optimize its performance internally, it is important to look beyond values and to include all the levels on which an organization operates. This tool helps you to compare where the organizational culture is now with where you want it to be in the future.

- *Scale*: decide on the scale of the exercise you wish to engage in:
  - just think things through on your own;
  - with a few colleagues (3–6 people);
  - with your management team or with a syndicate comprised of a vertical cross-section of your organization (5–15 people);
  - with a number of syndicates from across the organization (10–100 people);
  - with your organization, customers, suppliers and investors (outside facilitation of this process would be essential);

- *Present state*: Collect data on each logical level concerning the present state of the organization. Use the following prompt questions:

Context: the larger picture to which we contribute
- What does the organization belong to beyond its boundaries?
- How does the organization contribute to the wider community?

Identity: the vision, where we want to be
- What is our vision? What is the dream that we are trying to make happen? Do we have a BHAG?
- How excited are people about the vision?

Identity: our purpose
- What is our mission or role?
- What is our special contribution?

Beliefs
- How far do we believe in ourselves as an organization?
- How far do we believe in our capability to do something really worthwhile?
- How much do we believe in the value of our products?

Values
- What are the values we demonstrate in terms of how we do business?
- What are the values we demonstrate in terms of how we treat people?
- What are the values we demonstrate in terms of product quality?

Capabilities
- How competent are we at what we do?
- How competent are we at leadership?
- How competent are we at management?
- How well do we do what we do?
    The quality of our service?
    The quality of our products?
    Are our services/products 'state of the art' or behind the times?

Behaviours
- What sort of behaviours do we exhibit towards each other?
- Are these behaviours consistent with our vision and values?

Environment
- Is our working environment and the environment in which we deal with our customers consistent with our vision, mission and values?

- *Desired state*: build a common picture of the desired state on each logical level.

- *Synthesize*: summarize and integrate the data for present state and the desired state, being careful to consider weak signals (see Chapter 2).

- *Alignment actions*: determine what you might do to take the organization from present state to desired state. At this point it could be useful to create a syndicate of experts in the following areas to plan the initiatives:
  - compensation and benefits;
  - recruitment;
  - management development;
  - technical training;
  - organization development;
  - internal communication;
  - business consulting.

- *Implementation decision*: do you want to implement any or all of the plan? If so, which parts of the plan will generate most value to the organization?

- *Implementation*: if 'yes' to implementation, create a timing plan with milestones to implement the change programme. Regularly review the programme for any in-course correction required (see Chapter 8).

2. Encouraging rogue monkeys

How can you encourage more free-thinkers, people who are willing to bend the rules and challenge assumptions to help the organization meet its visionary objectives?

One way to do this is to select people who have a natural predisposition to think things through for themselves, challenge the status quo and take action.

In Chapter 5 we described a number of 'thinking styles', or metaprogrammes – ways we process information and interact with the world. Some of these thinking styles are indicators of entrepreneurial skills and an ability to innovate (Table 6.1).

Table 6.1   *Thinking styles as indicators of entrepreneurial skill and innovative ability*

Thinking styles category	Dimensions					
Approach to goals	Towards the goal			Away from the problem		
Locus of control	Proactive – self-referenced			Reactive – 'other' referenced		
Approach to tasks	Options and choices			Following procedures		
Time frame		Past—present—future				
Mode of comparison	Similarity			Difference		
Focus of interest	People	Activities	Places	Things	Information	Time

Entrepreneurs and innovators are likely to be oriented 'towards the goal'. In other words, they are more likely to describe their aims as achieving a result, such as market share growth or improved return on investment, rather than preventing a problem, such as reducing breakdowns, curbing cost increases or decreasing the risk of losing key staff.

Their locus of control is likely to be their own internal judgement. That is to say, they pay more attention to their own criteria for success than other people's opinions, and are therefore proactive about making things happen in the world, even if they meet resistance.

In terms of their approach to existing procedures, they are likely to be much more options oriented. That is to say, they are much more interested in finding the best way of doing something than following the existing procedure or method.

Entrepreneurs and innovators focus more on the future than on the past and the present: they ask themselves 'How do we get there?' rather than 'Where have we come from and what have we learned from past experience?'

They also look for different and new ideas, rather than ones that are similar to existing ones. Depending on their degree of interpersonal skill, they may appear confrontational in their search for new ideas.

If the potential change agent is activities (task) oriented, they are likely to deliver and get things done, but if they lack people orientation, you may need to soothe ruffled feathers. If they are people oriented, they are likely to try to get things done without making too many waves, but may avoid difficult decisions involving people. If they are place oriented, their attention will be on the way the physical environment can hinder or stimulate action. If they are information oriented, they will gather lots of data, but may be less predisposed to act on it. Gathering the information is what excites them.

Use your understanding of metaprogrammes to select and encourage informal or formal change agents. Pick a short-list of people and assess their metaprogrammes. This can be done informally by observing these distinctions in their behaviour, or by more formal profiling.

Use logical levels to plan how you coach the change agents.

- *Behaviour*: don't tell them what to do, or they won't act like rogue monkeys.
- *Capabilities*: don't define the tools they should use, but set them an overall objective or mission. Give them a BHAG or simply let them loose and see what they come up with in the broad area of the company mission. Define the limits of their powers. Develop good communication with them so they have an open channel to you. Review regularly, using in-course correction (see Chapter 8).
- *Beliefs*: validate the hell out of them. Tell them to take risks and that you will support them. Let them know that you believe in them and get them to believe in you. When the boat starts to rock, make sure you are watching their backs.
- *Identity*: sponsor *who they are*. Endorse and encourage their individualism. The more they feel that you support and understand who they are, the more they will want to give their very best.

- *Context*: find out what they want to contribute to the world and how this could add value in your organization.

3. Creating catalytic mechanisms

Catalytic mechanisms can be powerful enablers in liberating your organization to act effectively. Use this checklist to generate your own, customized mechanisms.

- *Brainstorm obstacles to the vision*: brainstorm a list of things in your organization that inhibit or block you from achieving your vision, desired organizational culture or strategic objectives.
- *Select an obstacle to explore*: select an issue that involves people inside your organization. Choose an area where you have the power to set policy or the ability to influence the people who do.
- *Brainstorm potential catalytic mechanisms*: brainstorm a list of outrageous mechanisms that would eliminate the obstacle. Adapt the principle that 'any idea is a good idea'. If you are brainstorming with colleagues, encourage each other to come up with absurd, wild and perhaps even dangerous ideas of mechanisms that will bypass hierarchy, bureaucracy and the typical rules and procedures that are blocking you.
- *Conduct a SWOT analysis on potential mechanisms*: pick likely candidates from your list and conduct a SWOT analysis on each one:
  - What are the strengths of the idea?
  - What are the weaknesses?
  - What opportunities are there to realize this mechanism?
  - What might sabotage or undermine the mechanism?
- *Try out the idea on key stakeholders and implement if appropriate.*

For more resources on creating cultures that can act, see
www.AlphaLeaders.com

Conclusion

Cultures that can act have three distinctive qualities. They are clear, but adaptable. They not only tolerate dissent, they encourage it, because they see it as both a source of novelty and an antidote to the inappropriate and outdated assumptions and mental models that tend to accumulate within, and constrain, less open cultures. Finally, they are always on the lookout for feedback mechanisms that enhance their adaptability and responsiveness and maintain their openness.

Such cultures are rare because it is hard to maintain cultural strength and clarity while indulging mavericks and subversives. Catalytic mechanisms are very useful when developing such cultures, because they make flexibility an integral part of the culture, rather than a separate quality that a leader has to maintain deliberately.

Alignment is critical, but without timely and effective action, it is nothing. In the following three chapters, we will explore the final component of Alpha Leadership: Act.

References

1. 3M website at http://www.mmm.com.
2. Bartlett, C. and Ghoshal, S. (1999) *The Individualized Corporation*, Heinemann.
3. 3M website at http://www.mmm.com.
4. Cinematrix, Interactive Entertainment Systems at www.cinematrix.com.
5. Roberts, K. (2000) *CEO Exchange: International Branding in the 21st Century*, WWCI/Chicago broadcast, Episode 105, October.
6. Collins, J. and Porras, J. (1994) *Built to Last: Successful Habits of Visionary Companies*, Harper Business.
7. Kunde, J. (2000) *Corporate Religion*, Pearson Education.
8. Roberts, K. (2000) Op. cit.
9. Warner, J. (2001) Can she do the business? *The Independent*, 20 October.
10. Thompson, J.D. (1967) *Organizations in Action*, McGraw-Hill.
11. Roberts, K. (2000) Op. cit.
12. Collins, J. (1999) Turning goals into results: the power of catalytic mechanisms, *Harvard Business Review*, July–August.

Part III

Act

Knowledge is only a rumour until it's in the muscle.

Papua New Guinean proverb

What we do matters. Whether putting our organizations' carefully designed plans into practice, or constructing our own working day, action is, in the end, the only thing that counts. How often have we experienced meetings that only lead to other meetings; strategies viewed and reviewed, but never implemented; teams circling in analysis paralysis, unable to break through into effective action?

We are not talking about initiating a 'let's look busy' culture, where we all run around like headless chickens. We are campaigning for action that is securely founded on the anticipation and alignment described in Parts I and II.

In the three chapters of Part I we demonstrated how leaders can increase their own and their organizations' ability to *anticipate* by constructing sensory systems able to detect 'weak signals', by using their mental agility to see the opportunities and threats implied by the signals and by liberating the self-organizing power latent in all complex systems.

In Part II we explained how you as a leader can *align* your organization, by embodying your goals and beliefs, by acting as a catalyst for creativity and effective work by managing relationships rather than undertaking tasks, and by developing and nurturing a coherent, action-oriented culture.

We now turn, in Part III, to the question of how good leaders *act*. Act comes last, not because action can be left until last, but because it needs to *anticipate* events and the organization must *align* behind it, if it is to be effective.

Effective action has three essential components. Prioritizing tasks and focusing on where we can add most value is the first step towards eliminating the feelings of stress and overload many of us are experiencing. Have you ever had a sinking feeling when you log on to discover 80 e-mails demanding your attention? Do you dread going on holiday because of the work backlog that will be waiting for you on your return? Do you finish the day wondering how you can have been so frenetically busy achieving so little? Then read on – Chapter 7, 80:20 Leadership, is for you.

The second element of effective action is to be more interested in speed than direction, and to rely on the timely use of 'in-course correction'. The approaches described in Chapter 8, Ready, Fire, Aim, can reduce frustration and wasted effort by breaking through log jams, particularly where these are caused by the organization's reluctance to act until a perfect solution has been found.

Finally, in Chapter 9, Dogged Pursuit, we address the subtle difference between persistence and stubbornness, and the vital importance of knowing when to stop. The impact on you, the business leader, is likely to be the winning back of valuable time to use more effectively, whether at work or at home.

Once again, each of the three chapters will end with tools designed to help ensure that you and your organization act swiftly and effectively.

7

80:20 Leadership

First things first.

Proverbs

Stephen Covey recounts the story of an instructor lecturing on time.[1]

> At one point the instructor said, 'Okay, it's time for a quiz.' He reached under the table and pulled out a wide-mouth gallon jar. He set it on the table next to a platter with some fist-sized rocks on it. 'How many of those rocks do you think we can get in the jar?' he asked.
>
> After we made our guess, he said, 'Okay, let's find out.' He set one rock in the jar . . . then another . . . then another. I don't remember how many he got in, but he got the jar full. Then he asked, 'Is that jar full?'
>
> Everybody looked at the rocks and said 'Yes.'
>
> Then he said 'Ahhh.' He reached under the table and pulled out a bucket of gravel. Then he dumped some gravel in and shook the jar and the gravel went in all the little spaces left by the big rocks. Then he grinned and said once more, 'Is the jar full?'
>
> By this time we were on to him. 'Probably not,' we said.
>
> 'Good!' he replied. And he reached under the table and brought out a bucket of sand. He started dumping the sand in and it went in all the little spaces left by the rocks and the gravel. Once more he looked at us and said, 'Is the jar full?' 'No!' we all roared.
>
> He said, 'Good!' and he grabbed a pitcher of water and began to pour it in. He got something like a quart of water in that jar. Then he said, 'Well, what's the point?'
>
> Somebody said, 'Well, there are gaps, and if you really work at it, you can always fit more into your life.'
>
> 'No,' he said, 'that's not the point. The point is this: if you hadn't put these big rocks in first, would you ever have gotten any of them in?'

This is a well-known story, but one that is worth repeating. It is a salutary reminder that the rocks, the most important tasks of leadership, must go in first, because otherwise the available space will get filled up with less productive tasks. In other words, the leader's time must be allocated around the tasks that add most of the leader's value.

The pebbles, gravel and sand are important too, but they are very seductive and can keep people in leadership positions so busy, they have no time for the defining tasks of leadership, such as weak signal detection, relationship management and coaching. This is one of the reasons why many able managers underperform when they are promoted to leadership positions. They have the technical competence they need to be promoted to leadership positions, but they get caught in what Covey calls 'the thick of thin things', and they struggle to acquire a leader's wider perspective.[2]

Before we tell you how you can get more rocks in the jar, we should explain why this self-evidently desirable goal of spending the bulk of your time on the high-value-added tasks of leadership is so hard to achieve. We all know it is vital, and we keep telling ourselves we must make time for long-term thinking, but we don't do it.

In much the same way as we know we need to take exercise to stay fit, we know we need to consume fewer calories to stay slim, and we know we need to floss daily to keep our teeth, there seems to be a gap between knowledge and action in prioritizing our working lives – a gap in which our good intentions evaporate. We all know we need to focus on the priority tasks, but how many times have you found your day slipping away from you, lost in a morass of urgent 'stuff'?

The way leaders manage and allocate their time has long been recognized as a crucial issue, and much has been written about it. But despite all the exhortations in the extensive time management literature, it is very difficult, particularly for detail-oriented people, to distinguish and strike the perfect balance between 'doing things right', and 'doing the right things'. We seem to be victims of some kind of natural law that entangles us inextricably in the details and trivia of the moment.

We *are* victims of a law – and it's called the 80:20 law. Whatever area of human endeavour we consider, it always transpires that 80% of the effort produces 20% of the benefit. Or, in other words, 20% of the effort produces 80% of the benefit. If only we could identify and bolster that 20% . . .

In human rather than statistical terms, we tend to do the things we're good at or familiar with and, because we are members of working communities, we let other people put their rocks in our jars. We have to get control of our own schedules because, unless we make deliberate efforts to dispense with or delegate the unimportant tasks, they will gradually come, pebble by pebble, to dominate our working day, as the following example shows.

While coaching the quality director of a major teaching hospital, it quickly became clear that her 80:20 was going to be hard to identify. She was frantically busy, constantly besieged by requests for her time both from within the hospital and from patients and their relatives. The job was not only physically and mentally exhausting, but often also exerted a heavy emotional strain. Each day started two hours before her direct reports and finished well after midnight. Meetings ran back to back, leaving no time to implement any actions agreed in those meetings. As a result, the typical outcome of each meeting was to set up yet another meeting. A deputy director had been appointed to relieve some of the workload, but there was no time to train him, or sometimes even to talk to him, in a day full of the demands of others.

The starting point in breaking out of this cycle was to step back from the day-to-day and to look again at the director's objectives. These fell into three main areas of service delivery. It was then a relatively easy task to allocate the million and one activities filling her day against these three categories. Anything that didn't fit was examined for its value to the organization as a whole, and if it didn't add value, it was dropped. As a result of this exercise, she calculated that less than 15% of her day was dedicated to activities that progressed her own agenda – 85% was eaten up in the urgency of others.

Turning this insight into action required persistence and resourcefulness. The main challenge was to take proactive control of how the director spent her time, and importantly, to build in dedicated sessions to work with the deputy, training him and delegating to him a variety of critical tasks. Core activities that were taking up a lot of time needed to be reviewed for how they could become more efficient. For example, writing replies to letters of complaint was a time-consuming process that went through many tedious iterations. Stepping back and doing something about the process itself was tough since it took yet more precious time away from handling the pressing tasks of today. However, by reengineering the process of complaints handling, the director managed to release significant amounts of time over the next few months: an investment in the present paid dividends in the future.

As this story demonstrates, there are three options. We can dispense with the non-essential tasks, delegate them or be overwhelmed by them. Make no mistake: if you don't choose options one or two, then option three will choose you.

This chapter offers you some tools and approaches to help you to identify the 20%, to allocate time and resources accordingly, delegating some of the 80%, and to take a new perspective on time so you can plan more effectively.

For people who recognized the role described in our introduction as 'VP of long hours and no fun', this is for you. This is the part that will help you get your life back.

Identify the 20%

Marketing people used to say that although they knew half of the money they spent on advertising was wasted, they did not know which half. It was this inherent wastefulness of advertising that led to the growth of 'below-the-line' marketing activities, such as promotions, public relations and direct mail. Marketing professionals are always searching for 'more bang for their marketing buck' in an endless quest for an unattainable perfection when not a penny of their budgets will be wasted.

Leaders also need to search for the unattainable: that perfect set of tasks only they can do, that will not waste a moment of their time. This may seem rather optimistic, but the process of trying to achieve this goal will in itself make you more effective, even if you never quite get there.

It is not a matter of ignoring the detail altogether and concentrating all your time and energy on 'leadership' tasks. As we saw in Chapter 4 you have to remain involved in the detail, to some extent, to maintain your relationships, your expertise and your 'feel' for the current priorities, but you must avoid getting stuck in the details. You have to be a doer and a dreamer – in the detail and beyond the detail – at the same time.

There are some practical tools you can use to detect and exploit the 20%. We will describe them briefly here and in more detail in the Tools for Thought section at the end of this chapter. But first it is important to pause and reflect on the thinking style, the 'metaprogramme', you bring to this task, since this will radically affect the ease with which you find that elusive 20%.

Remember the concentric circles of leadership we looked at in Chapter 4? The inner circle represented technical competence, and the outer ring represented leadership. We pointed out that when the leadership ring is narrow, and the technical competence circle is wide, the leader gets lost in the detail. If you are a details person, you should delegate to make room for more rocks. If you are a 'vision' person, with a narrow competence 'core', you should get more involved in the details to make sure you are choosing the right rocks (see Figure 4.1).

Take a moment to reflect on how you see the world. Do you tend to spot the small points, the detail behind the big picture? Are you the person in the room who brings the conversation around to practicalities and specifics; who notices, for example, that the solution won't work in three regional plants because they have a different configuration? If so, recognize that you process information in small chunks, and that it will require an effort to step back and see the overall picture. Make a conscious effort to divide your assessment of the situation into bigger chunks, broader pictures and more holistic interpretations. Seek the support of a 'big chunk' colleague in applying the tools described here.

All leaders must stretch objectives and actions in order to achieve continuous improvement and attain results. The key, however, is to stretch the right things and in the right areas. The old adage, that we need to work smarter not harder, has never been truer than in today's hectic workplace. In this regard, stretching needs to be combined with *vision*, so that stretching is aligned with longer term value creation and not focused on arbitrary objectives. There needs to be a balance between vision and achievement.

Although leadership tasks vary from time to time and from industry to industry, there are some tasks that almost always constitute the leader's 20%.

1. *Self management.* Top of the list is the attention the leader pays to him or herself; ensuring he or she is personally in alignment, as we described in Chapter 4; taking care to step back from the day-to-day and focus on high leverage activities; and taking care of his or her own emotional health and wellbeing. One CEO of a European professional services firm takes time every Thursday morning to play tennis with his wife. He works long and hard throughout the rest of the week, and, as he says, you can always find a few hours to do what is right for yourself and your family.

2. *From vision to market.* It goes without saying that articulating visions and formulating strategies are prerogatives of the leader, because it is clearly

impossible to decide what other tasks belong exclusively to you, as the leader, until you have a pretty clear idea of where you are going.

Holding 'big pictures' in your mind of the external marketplace and of the organization as a 'system' within it, is also a necessary prerequisite for developing the anticipation skills we described in Part I. It will be hard to decide, for example, what 'weak signals' you should pay attention to and focus your mental agility on, unless you have clear objectives and at least a general idea of where your organization as a whole is now, or might become capable of.

Whether you call it a vision, mission or strategy, an organization needs to know where it is going, and why, and it is your responsibility as leader to set that course and get that purpose 'into the muscle' of the organization. Purposes are the products of possibilities and potentials. You will only be able to spot the possibilities if you understand the external system, and you will only be able to help the organization realize its potential if you understand the internal system and the nature of your influence within it.

3. *Managing key relationships.* Among the most important agents in your 'internal system' are what might be called your 'upward stakeholders' – your immediate boss, others both within and outside the organization who have direct authority over you and, in the case of CEOs and other senior executives, the board and shareholders. It is your responsibility to manage your part of the organization's relationships with such powerful agents within whose gift lie the resources, freedoms and support you need to achieve your goals.

You need to understand and work out how to help them further their agendas and the agendas of *their* upward stakeholders, and the purposes you embed 'in the muscle' of your part of the organization must be, if not shaped by, at least compatible with theirs. As leader, you are your organization's chief ambassador and negotiator with other parts of the wider system and, as such, you need to develop diplomatic skills and learn to use them effectively to build powerful coalitions to get things done.

4. *Organizational alignment.* A critical, and often neglected, leadership task is the mobilization of the organization to act in concert to deliver strategic goals. Aligned organizations *learn*, and behind every 'learning organization' lie teacher–leaders. Teaching leads to empowerment, and when the leader teaches – when 'teacher' becomes one of the roles the leader

embodies (see Chapter 4) – a wavefront of empowerment can cascade down through the organization, and supercharge its capabilities.

On-the-job coaching, or 'action learning', requires a one-to-one, apprentice–master relationship. Learning contracts are personal trades. People are much more likely to do what you ask of them, to the best of their abilities, and in the spirit of the corporate vision, if you help them to become more capable. Leaders cannot coach everyone, but they can coach and develop their direct reports, and, in doing so, can establish traditions of coaching and mentoring for alignment throughout the organization.

5. *Key systems and resources.* The final task area is to identify and ensure that the organization has what it needs to succeed. It involves aligning your systems – technical and social – to your goals, and ensuring that your resources are sufficiently flexible to respond quickly to changes in the environment.

Few would dispute that these generic task areas are the prerogatives and responsibilities of the leader, but few make specific time to undertake them. If they are to be carried out effectively, you will need to allocate a specific proportion of your time to them. Do you?

These then are the generic tasks of leadership, but how can you identify the leadership tasks specific to the time and the circumstances? Bear in mind, if you do not define your rocks and get them in the jar right away, there may be no room for them later.

Step back from the day-to-day and remind yourself of your overarching objectives. Look at your tasks and chunk right the way up to your overall goal. Do the tasks connect to your objectives? Are there some objectives without supporting tasks? Are there discretionary tasks that could be dispensed with or delegated?

Covey uses a powerful phrase as an additional prompt to unearth rocks. He suggests we ask ourselves, 'What one thing could you do in your personal and professional life that, if you did it on a regular basis, would make a tremendous positive difference in your life?'[3] When you have answered this question, ensure you make time for this activity.

Malcolm Graveling, an A.T. Kearney colleague, uses another useful approach to surface important and perhaps neglected rocks. He calls this the Golden Hour test. Ask yourself if you had one extra hour in the day how would you spend it? Having answered this question, now make sure you do this for the first hour of every day.

Allocate resources accordingly

Having found the 20%, the next critical step is to allocate time and resources according to the priorities identified. This often requires a real paradigm shift from reactive to proactive, positively scheduling the critical activities, rather than hoping you can somehow fit them in. Again, this is not rocket science and these are familiar concepts. Putting them into practice, however, is often a different matter.

The portfolio of activities which express an organization's vision and values cannot be enacted mechanically or reactively in response to changing circumstances. Rather they must be put into action consistently through time. Time allocation is where 'the rubber meets the road' with respect to values. In a very real way, what a person spends his or her time doing is the most direct expression of his or her values (even if the person is not consciously aware of those values). How you choose to allocate time transmits strong messages about what matters to you. For example, if you say the customer comes first, and yet you spend less than 10% of your time with customers, your organization hears the message loud and clear – customers don't really come first. In fact they come a poor fourth after internal budgetary issues, staff meetings and e-mails.

John Chambers transmitted a powerful message about his priorities when he arrived half an hour late for his first board meeting as chief executive of Cisco Systems, because he insisted on solving a client problem first.

Take the chunked up tasks and goals you have identified. Look at where you want to spend time and in what proportion. Now spend some time with a time diary. Make a rough assessment of where you actually spend your time. How does it compare? Where do you want to make adjustments, to add time or take it away? Now spend the next week doing just that. This will require you to take control of your agenda, to time key activities and ensure that you proactively plan your diary to accommodate core activities and to block out others. Critically, it will require you to implement the options described above – to dispense with non-essential activities and to delegate others.

The dispensing option is easily dispensed with. Whenever a task you suspect adds no value comes at you, don't do it. You can't be sure, particularly if you are new to the job, that a task is unnecessary, but by not doing it, you are testing its importance. If you don't do it and nothing untoward happens, it's probably a habit you or your predecessor acquired for reasons that were valid at the time, but which no longer apply. One automotive assembler estimated that, of the hundreds of reports generated for management, less than 10% of them were ever read, and still fewer had any impact on decision making.

Delegation is more difficult, but it is a much more powerful weapon in your efforts to skew the distribution curve of your tasks to the high end of the importance scale.

The mechanics of delegation

Delegation is an important theme of our times. You can see it in the growth of outsourcing, subcontracting, partnerships and alliances. Organizations no longer feel compelled to do everything themselves. They know that, these days, there are plenty of organizations that can do some of the things they used to do just as well as them, if not better. So they have replaced tasks they used to do themselves with relationships, and in so doing have improved their efficiency and lowered their costs of doing business.

So far, we have been talking about a 'task' as a coherent unit of work with one or more relationships attached to it. But tasks can be subdivided into goals (what we are trying to achieve), and means (the way of achieving those goals). Once you analyse tasks in these terms, you will start to see opportunities for partial delegation.

It is helpful to think of delegation options as lying on a spectrum ranging from minimal delegation at one end, where you continue to dictate both goal and means, to total delegation at the other, where you surrender control of goal *and* means (see Figure 7.1). In between these two poles are two intermediate options we call 'negotiation' and 'facilitation'. In 'negotiation' you keep control of the goal and reach agreement on means with those to whom you're delegating. In 'facilitation' you again keep control of the goal, but you withdraw even further from the means, by merely ensuring that those to whom you are delegating have the resources they need for the means they choose.

Sometimes you can go the whole hog, and allow delegates to control the goal too, or that part of it not incorporated in other goals or means under

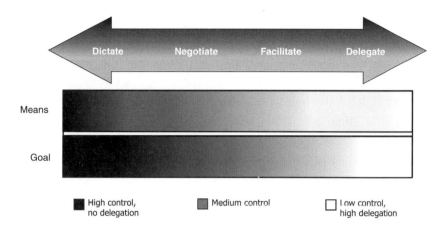

Figure 7.1 *The spectrum of delegation*

your direct control. But more often you will want to keep your eye on things and reserve the right to intervene if the relevant performance indicators start to move in the wrong direction.

We saw in Chapter 3 how self-organizing processes can 'emerge' from a few simple rules. Performance indicators are simple rules, in the sense that an intervention in the process they measure is only triggered when they stray beyond preset limits. In such cases, control of the goal is delegated to a system, while control of the means is delegated to a person.

The art of delegation

It is not enough to know the delegation options and understand how they can be applied to a particular case. Delegation has a psychological, as well as a mechanical dimension, because it involves getting other people to do work you used to do. They have to be willing, or preferably eager, to take on the new task, and it is up to you to cultivate that eagerness.

The first step is to encourage a sharing of agendas, including your own. It is in the interests of your colleagues that you perform well as the leader, because a good team performance enhances the reputation of each member. But your staff may not realize the extent to which they are preventing you from doing the leader's job. Sharing agendas and making sure everyone knows your priorities are diplomatic ways of saying: 'don't put your rocks in my jar'.

In risk-averse cultures, 'aggregate' (sand, gravel and pebbles) moves up the hierarchy, as those lower down pass on responsibilities to those higher up. The rocks of the former become the pebbles of the latter, and there is less and less room for rocks at any level. You have to reverse the direction. In vibrant, creative, empowered cultures, aggregate moves downwards. Pebbles in the jars of those above become rocks in the jars of those below, and there is more room for rocks at every level.

Most people are keen to stretch themselves, assume new responsibilities and face new challenges, but, at the same time, no one likes being 'dumped on'. As you take pebbles from your jar, and make them rocks in the jars of other people, you have to 'sell' the rocks. You have to make people feel they are being entrusted with a task that will give them valuable experience, rather than being lumbered with a chore. It is not hard to do. People tend to take a positive view, and it is easy for them to feel that taking on the leader's tasks is part of their career development. When you ask someone to do some strategy development work for you, for example, he or she will have to talk to members in your peer group, and will be exposed to a higher level of the organization. It will feel like practice, like preparation for promotion.

This is the apprentice–master model. The great Renaissance painters did not do all the work themselves. They painted the outlines and key features, got the proportions right and told their apprentices (some of whom would later become masters themselves) to fill in the gaps. A technique used in animation known as 'storyboarding' exemplifies the same principle. The head animator does the key expression and movement frames and leaves juniors to complete the rest of the picture sequence. Great chefs are similar. They do not cook anything – they taste what their assistants cook, and if it is not right, they bin it, and tell the assistant to do it again, using a bit more salt or a little less saffron.

Delegation not only helps you to make room in your jar for more rocks. It is also your most important tool when you are discharging your duty to develop your direct reports.

Competence and motivation are the key factors in delegation. People who are neither competent nor motivated would be better working somewhere else, but people who lack competence can be trained, and those who lack enough hunger for new challenges can be motivated.

When trying to judge what motivates particular people, ask yourself whether they appear to running away from, or towards something. Watch out for those who seem to be running away – they will be trying to put their rocks in your jar. Those who are running towards something (to the time when they will be leaders themselves perhaps) will be eager to take your pebbles. If they are also competent, all that remains is for you to give them the resources they need to do the job.

Time

When John Egan was transforming Jaguar Cars (now part of Ford) in the early 1980s, one of the tasks he set himself was to 'get the timing right', as he put it. The car market had a rhythm to it, created by the peaks and troughs of seasonal demand. Previously, Jaguar had worked to its own manufacturing rhythm, and never had enough cars in stock to satisfy demand at the seasonal peaks. Egan took on the job of Jaguar's chief timekeeper and aligned the company's internal rhythm with that of its market.

Leaders must take charge of time and timing in their organizations. To do so effectively, you need to be aware of your own attitude to time. Your relationship to time represents another aspect of the way we process information, another 'metaprogramme' we run as we try to make sense of the world.

It may appear odd to be discussing time at this point. Surely time is a given, a set distribution of seconds, minutes and hours that divide up our lives? But time is not always what it seems. We all experience time differently, depending on the way we process information, and the way we relate to time. In fact, Ricardo Quinones maintains that time as a concept was really only discovered during the Renaissance. Prior to that era, Quinones describes a society with little consciousness of the passing of hours and days, a society that confidently launched cathedral building projects that lasted centuries, well beyond the lifetimes of the architects and builders.[4] Time, then, is an elastic concept, open to a number of different interpretations, each of which will affect our ability to focus on the 20%.

Time lines have various shapes, and studies have shown that people see time in different ways depending on their situations and roles, as well as their personal predispositions. People involved in mechanical operations, such as production, for example, tend to see time as linear, whereas R&D people tend to see time in bits and pieces, that come together to form a pattern when a critical cusp point is reached.

If you tend to live in the moment and focus your attention on events unfolding right now, your relationship to time is known as 'in time'. You tend to live in the now, enjoying the moment and often forgetting upcoming commitments or deadlines. There is much to be said for being in time. It makes you less anxious about the future and less prone to brood about the past, and it is often associated with creativity, mental agility, a willingness to experiment and good interpersonal skills. You often arrive late for meetings, however, and you tend to be unwilling to plan.

If this is a fair description of you, in applying the tools we describe here you will need consciously to develop a planning habit, or find a partner who lives 'through time' to help you and act as your coach.

John Egan – one of the most admired UK business leaders of the 1980s – saw things 'through time'. He distanced himself from the now, and saw the present in relationship to the past and the future. He was a good planner, and as his alignment of Jaguar's annual rhythm with the annual rhythm of the marketplace showed, he understood that important time lines could be cyclical as well as linear.

'Through time' individuals tend to have a good sense of the future, and can more easily relate activities they undertake in the present to future outcomes or other competing needs. They will rarely find themselves running late or missing appointments because they have become engrossed in reading or discussing something. The downside of being 'through time' is that it can be hard to focus on the moment and truly enjoy it, without worrying about what comes next. It can prove difficult giving people the attention they need, since the conflicting demands of what came before and what comes after tend to get in the way.

If this is a fair description of you, in applying the tools we describe here be careful not to overplan, to become too rigid in your scheduling. Leave white space to explore and deal with the unexpected. Find a partner who lives 'in time' to help you live in the moment, to focus on the tasks in the present and to act as your coach.

In the end, of course, the 80:20 dilemma is all about time – about the time you, as a leader, spend on genuine leadership tasks. Most rocks have longer time lines, or 'half-lives' as nuclear physicists would say, than pebbles. They are often relatively easy to neglect, because they are not urgent, but as they sit there, next to your glass jar, side-lined by pebbles and sand, they are emitting radiation that is gradually poisoning your organization's potential.

Tools for thought

1. Identifying the 20%: prioritizing tasks

The following tool provides a way to explore and identify initiatives that are likely to be the most significant and have the greatest leverage in reaching longer term results.

On the left-hand side of Table 7.1, list the initiatives you want to prioritize or from which you must select. Then, rate the degree to which each initiative fits (high, medium or low) with respect to the six decision criteria listed across the top of the table:

- *Mission critical.* How significant is the initiative with respect to the mission of your group or organization?
- *Congruent with key values.* How fully does the initiative match the key values of your group or organization?
- *Matches core competence.* To what extent does the initiative fit with the core competence of your group or organization?
- *Fits with critical success factors.* How well does the initiative meet key success factors (e.g. clear need, adequate sponsorship, buy in from stakeholders, visible feedback, etc.)?
- *Degree of pay-off.* What is the potential pay-off resulting from the initiative?
- *Amount of cost/risk.* How much cost or risk is associated with the initiative?

Table 7.1 *Prioritizing tasks*

Initiatives	Decision criteria					
	Mission critical	Congruent with key values	Matches core competence	Fits with CSFs	Degree of payoff	Amount of cost/risk

One quick way to tally your results is to assign a number (3–high, 2–medium, 1–low) for each ranking (make the number associated with cost/risk a negative number) and add them up. Look at the overall scores and assess where to focus your attention.

If run as a group workshop, this exercise can be a powerful way to gain agreement and commitment where there are differences of opinion on priorities.

2. Allocating resources: values planning

As we said previously, how you choose to allocate time is an important message about what matters to you and your organization. Your colleagues will judge the integrity of what you say you value according to the time you allocate to the activities that manifest your values in the workplace.

The following tool will help you determine the amount of time you allocate to the portfolio of activities that converts your values into practice. List the activities that best express the values to be implemented. Make up a time allocation worksheet like the one shown in Figure 7.2. Write the list of activities in the spaces in the middle of the worksheet. On the pie chart on the right, under the column Desired state, represent the percentage of time you will need to allocate to each activity if the values are to be successfully established.

Now review what you have specified as the allocation you would like, and compare it to the time you actually spend on these activities. Using the pie chart on the left-hand side of the worksheet, represent the relative amounts of time you are currently spending with respect to each activity.

Do the same with the second half of the worksheet. List the people with whom you are collaborating in order to undertake these activities. Note the proportion of your time you would *like* to spend with them in order to be successful in your activities, and note this on the right side of the worksheet. Compare these percentages with the time you *actually* spend with each individual, noted on the left side of the worksheet.

Remember, optimally you would be spending the majority of your time with the individuals and activities that produce 80% of the results. What activities would you reduce or cut out? Increase? With whom would you need to spend more time? Less time? And what do you need to do to make this happen?

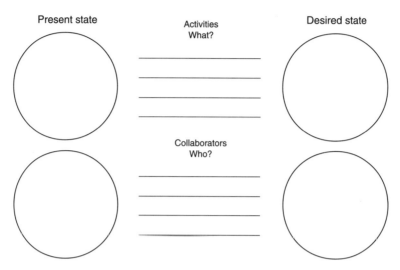

Present state

Activities
What?

Desired state

Collaborators
Who?

Figure 7.2 *Time allocation worksheet*

3. Smart delegation

The CEO of a Swiss electrical products manufacturer was having problems with the structure of his organization. The company was highly matrixed, and moved slowly to respond to shifts in the market. Two product divisions were in direct competition in domestic markets due to changes in application technologies. Internal transfer pricing issues were making many core products uncompetitive by the time they reached the customer. The CEO tasked his direct reports to come up with solutions to these problems. He set up teams to study the issues and present him with recommendations.

After three months of hard work, the teams were looking forward to presenting their findings and recommended actions to the board. They had concluded that the two product-focused divisions should be merged, and that two new, customer-facing organizations to address the domestic and industrial markets with a full product offering should be established in their place.

Half an hour into their presentation, the CEO rose to his feet, brusquely announced that this was not the solution he was looking for, and left the room. The team was devastated, and morale never fully recovered.

It is easy to get delegation wrong. In this case, the CEO was clear what he was looking for and how to achieve it. He had underestimated the creativity of the team, assuming they would stick within the framework of the existing organization and come up with a minor adjustment to the current organization structure. The disappointment and unmet expectations on both sides had a long-term impact on the company, and could have been avoided if the delegation process had been properly negotiated.

We described the process of delegation in this chapter as a spectrum rather than a one-off event. The following tool is a helpful way of opening dialogue with your direct reports, and establishing a graphic contract for how the process of delegation is going to work. It will help make the delegation process more effective and will also avoid the catastrophic mismatch of expectations demonstrated in the case above.

There are three main factors to establish in terms of delegation: to what extent are you going to delegate the setting of goals? And to what extent are you going to delegate defining the means of achieving those goals? Finally, over what time frame will this take place?

Objective Owner: _____ Line Manager: _____ Date: _____

Key Area 1: _____

Goal

	Month 1	Month 2	Month 3	Month 4	Month 5	Month 6
Dictate	◯———	◯———	◯———	◯		
Negotiate					◯———	◯
Facilitate						
Delegate						

Means

	Month 1	Month 2	Month 3	Month 4	Month 5	Month 6
Dictate	◯———	◯				
Negotiate			◯———	◯		
Facilitate					◯	
Delegate						◯

Figure 7.3 *From dictate to delegate*

The framework shown in Figure 7.3 provides an example of a simple mechanism to stimulate dialogue around delegation. Identify an area of responsibility that you wish to delegate, and sit down with the individual or team that is going to take it on. Agree with them the extent to which you are going to pass responsibility to them. Are you going to dictate goals yourself? Are you going to negotiate goals? Will you facilitate the team in coming up with their own goals? Or leave it entirely up to them? Over what time frame will this take place? Ask the same questions for the means to achieve these goals. Will you dictate the means? Will you negotiate with them? Will you facilitate them to determine how to achieve their goals? Or leave it up to them? Over what time frame will you arrive at this level of delegation?

For both goals and means, establish as far as possible visible, tangible milestones which will indicate that you have stuck to the contract. Post the contract in a visible place and make sure you refer to it when issues arise.

For more resources on 80:20 leadership, go to www.AlphaLeaders.com

Conclusion

The key to effective working lies in putting into practice the power of the 80:20 rule – focusing on those activities that generate maximum value, and learning to delegate effectively those that do not. The main challenge is to find the energy and dedication to put these concepts into practice. This may in part come from having the discipline to stick to some of the techniques described in this chapter. However, as Covey points out, often the real problem people experience in organizing around priorities is that the priorities 'have not become deeply implanted in their hearts'.[5] If you feel that you lack energy to achieve your goals, take another look at the alignment approaches in Chapter 4. A truly aligned personal and business agenda will tap into deep reserves of dedication and commitment.

In the next chapter, we will focus on taking early action, the 'ready, fire, aim' approach to leadership.

References

1. Covey, S. (1994) *First Things First*, Simon and Schuster.
2. Covey, S. (1989) *The Seven Habits of Highly Effective People*, Simon and Schuster.
3. *Ibid.*
4. Quinones, R. (1973) *Renaissance Discovery of Time*, Harvard University Press.
5. Covey, S. (1989) *Op. cit.*

8

Ready, Fire, Aim

In skating over thin ice, our safety is in our speed.

Ralph Waldo Emerson

The astonishing accuracy of modern precision guided munitions was evident to everyone during the Gulf War and subsequent NATO actions in the Balkans. In the age of the gun, marksmen readied themselves, aimed their weapons, and then fired. In the age of the guided weapon, the aiming is often done after the launch, either remotely by a human targeter or by the weapon itself. You fire first and then you aim. It is a much better system because it allows weapon controllers to attack targets before they know where those targets will be at interception, and it empowers 'smart' weapons to follow their targets if the latter change course, and to adapt themselves to the changing circumstances of their missions.

Guns worked well when most targets were stationary. When targets responded to the increasing accuracy of guns by becoming more mobile, weapons responded by substituting guidance and in-course correction for aiming.

The constant competitive struggle between business organizations is also an evolutionary process. In this chapter we describe how the dynamics of business competition put leaders under the same pressure to abandon the traditional 'ready, aim, fire' approach, and to equip themselves and their organizations with the ability and reflexes to fire first, and ask questions about exactly where the target is later.

The IT director of a global consumer products company epitomized this approach at a recent meeting with his team when he said:

> Here's the problem. The business units want tailor-made software to give
> them information for a wide range of users: manufacturing, procurement,

customer service, HR, finance and senior management information requirements. No problem. And they want it in 18 months. Again, no problem, we
can run a project of this size on a tight time-scale and deliver. But in 18
months, the technology we are using to develop this application will be obsolete. And in 18 months, the market will have evolved, there will probably have
been another restructuring, and the users' needs will have changed. By the
time we have scoped, designed and implemented the project, it will already
be past its sell-by date.

Then he added:

Much of the software design and technical expertise we have in our division
is superfluous. We need to change how we operate, to buy rough and ready
software packages off the shelf, use them for a couple of years, and then throw
them away when the next phase of innovation comes along. The IT division is
no longer a group of technologists – we now manage business systems, buying and dumping technology as we keep reorientating to the next wave.

This IT director's vision for his team is a good example of the way companies will need to act in order to stay competitive. Many entrepreneurs
talk about the necessity of the *ready-fire-aim* strategy for building an emerging growth company, but in today's business climate it is not just the entrepreneurs who need these skills. Technology is advancing so rapidly that the
proposed specifications for a new product or service are likely to be out of
date before the project is completed. Regardless of the size or longevity of
your organization, be prepared. Take action on weak signals. Use in-course
corrections to improve what you are doing as you go.

Ready-fire-aim is the attempt to get something in front of the customer
as quickly as possible, get feedback, change and come back to the customer,
over and over again. As David Guo, CEO of Display Research Laboratories
and an avowed 'serial entrepreneur,' explains, 'Our strategy changes every
five minutes. Our vision and goal have not changed, but the strategy
changes every time there is new information.'[1]

Many companies seem to fall into one of two other categories: 'Aim-aim-
aim' or 'Fire-fire-fire'.

In companies adopting an aim-aim-aim approach, plans are perfectly
worked and perfectly designed, but the board or management team never
gets around to implementing them. It takes so long to develop a plan that,
by the time it has been developed, it is out of date and needs to be planned
again . . . and again . . . and again . . . .

In companies adopting a fire-fire-fire approach, management run round with their pants on fire, or at least gently smouldering, taking lots of action without any obvious vision or long-term strategic plan. These organizations are much too busy to plan, and the people within them suffer chronic initiative overload.

There is also a third category of firms that are very good at planning *and* very good at taking action, but the two activities don't connect with each other. These firms have annual strategic planning and budget cycles, but once the plan has been developed, it gets put on a shelf and left until the next annual cycle. The language used is normally vague, so that any progress at all will be considered satisfactory in a year's time. Meanwhile, management is running round taking care of short-term issues without any reference to the vision or the strategy.

Do any of these approaches sound familiar? How would you categorize your organization? Which category best fits the needs of your market?

This chapter is about cycling between effective preparation, quick-footed action, and regular review of progress against the strategic vision and strategic objectives – in other words, the three components of ready, fire, aim.

Ready

There has been much talk among military strategists recently about the need for 'fast reaction', or 'rapid deployment' forces, capable of defusing any potentially dangerous conflicts that develop anywhere in the world.

Fast reactions are vital in business too, and the state of 'being ready' is an essential prerequisite. You have to be clear about your overall goal, of course, and about which events and signals you need to respond to quickly, but clear goals and a deep understanding of the significance of events and 'weak signals' will be of no use if you are not ready.

We can build organizational readiness on two platforms: first, by establishing processes to provide evidence of the need to act, and second, by increased clarity around what constitutes readiness in each of the key dimensions of leadership.

Evidence drives action

Readiness is a state of mind, and has a lot to do with evidence. We saw, in our discussion of 'anticipation' in Part I, how smart sensory systems, and the mental agility needed to make sense of the weak signals they detect, are both important competitive advantages. Equally important, when it comes to action, are the evidence criteria and procedures that determine the trigger points for action.

Evidence takes two forms: final, bottom-line evidence, such as profit, that indicates whether a goal has or has not been achieved, and on-going, interim evidence, such as quality or innovation, that shows whether or not you are on track to achieve the goal. Final evidence is concerned with outcomes and the big picture and is 'in time'; on-going evidence deals with processes and details and is 'through time' (see Chapter 7 for more detail on these 'metaprogrammes').

Evidence 'procedures', such as quality tests, produce evidence. To be ready to act in good time when an innovation programme is falling behind schedule, for example, you need a clearly defined procedure to test the current state of the programme. These procedures need to be clear and accepted as fair and reasonable by everyone because they contribute to the whole organization's state of readiness. If there is debate about whether or not a goal has been achieved or is on track, or about whether the procedure that suggests it is behind schedule is fair, time will be wasted resolving the issue.

When setting up your evidence procedures, follow these guidelines:

1. State the goal of the procedure in positive terms. Give some examples of what 'good', rather than 'bad' outcomes would look like. Be as specific as possible.
2. Establish the purpose and benefits of the evidence procedure and make sure everyone understands why the evidence is necessary.
3. Connect evidence to observable patterns and cues so that there can be no dispute about whether or not the criteria have been met.
4. Make sure evidence procedures are easy to operate and maintain.
5. Establish time frames and milestones, so that evidence is produced at the right time and in the right form.
6. Anticipate problems. Be aware of situations in which people might object to the procedure or the context, and focus on the positive intentions behind such objections.

Your organization's evidence procedures are, in effect, the synapses of your organization's central nervous system, producing an early warning of the need to act.

It is important to be clear about the nature of 'decisive' evidence; that is to say, evidence that must be acted on right away. As we argued in Chapter 1, evidence does not have to be clear and unequivocal. It has to be credible, but it may be weak and ambiguous. Its decisiveness or otherwise lies not in its strength, but in its *implications* – in what it would mean, if it were true. Evidence that should be acted on right away often comes in the form of weak signals, and it is usually *more* decisive if it is weak, because signal weakness is a sign of earliness and, these days, the early birds get most of the worms.

Readiness of the 20%

To be ready for whatever wave comes our way, we need to look closely at the areas that generate most of our value as leaders (the 20% that provides 80% of our value).

In Chapter 7 we described five generic areas of '20%':

1. Self-management.
2. From vision to market.
3. Managing key relationships.
4. Organizational alignment.
5. Key systems and resources.

It is worth considering a series of simple questions when considering the extent to which you and your organization are ready to take on the challenges of rapid, iterative action. The perspective and insights of successful entrepreneurs, well used to ready-fire-aim businesses, also provide useful steers for leaders of more traditional organizations.

(1) Self-management

Business analysis will look at the shape of your business, and psychological assessment will look at you as a person – but conventional thinking rarely, if ever, makes a connection between these two perspectives. We believe, however, that the agility and intelligence of your business is largely determined by the emotional, psychological and physical wellbeing of you and your fellow leaders.

How aligned are you as a person (see Chapter 4)? What is your life balance like? How much energy do you have? If a major work challenge came along tomorrow, would you have the extra capacity to deal with it?

When you go into work in the morning, is there a spring in your step? If not, what are you doing about it? How ready are you for the next wave?

(2) From vision to market

Don Pickens is founder of Urban Design Online, Inc., former vice president and general manager of Connectix Corporation, and former group product manager at Microsoft Corporation for the $300 million Macintosh Office products division. Pickens advises that it is essential for entrepreneurs to 'stay focused and understand that your vision will differ from others who are looking at the same map'. He adds that, 'By definition an entrepreneur has a vision that is moving forward beyond what people are currently familiar or comfortable with.'

So what does readiness look like in this fluid area of leadership endeavour? Just like entrepreneur Pickens, ideally you will have a clear purpose, arrived at by looking at your products and chunking up (see Chapter 2) with the question, 'What does this achieve for the customer?' You will have a clear vision that the company is committed to achieving: strategic goals, and implementation plans for each of the strategic goals. Your day-to-day actions are driven by this plan, and you review it regularly to keep it up to date. It is a visible plan and everyone in the business understands it. Different people are personally accountable for different parts of the visionary plan, and its hierarchy of objectives, and these objectives are measurable. Performance is measured on the achievement of these objectives. Since culture and people development should be included in the plan, the managers' skills in these areas get measured, too.

(3) Managing key relationships

As one successful entrepreneur put it: 'You have to work with everybody, every day (your employees, your investors, etc.) to bring your vision together.'

Readiness in this area means that you know who your personal stakeholders are, and you have a plan for managing them. Your team knows who their stakeholders are, and you have a visible and shared plan for managing key stakeholders on behalf of the entire team.

(4) Organizational alignment

According to David Guo: 'A successful entrepreneur needs to be able to communicate his or her vision and ideas, and to understand people and their motivation.' He points out that you cannot *make* people do things. You have to get them to subscribe to your vision, and ask yourself, 'What motivates them to act?'

Guo maintains, 'My number one rule is always get people who are better than myself. Whoever you are hiring, make sure they are better than you.' This, of course, can create quite a challenge. Guo points out that he is often the youngest member of the team. He does not feel he can be their 'boss' or 'commander'. 'I respect my team,' he says. 'They have a lot more experience than I do, in many things. That's why I have them on my team. They know what I need better than I do. They don't need to come to me to ask for permission for things. My role as the leader of the company is to provide the necessary resources so they can best do their jobs.'[2]

Readiness in this area means having the right people and resources, doing the right things to fulfil the vision.

(5) Key systems and resources

Look at your organization from your customers' point of view. What affects the quality of their experience? How can your resources and systems be redesigned to be more likely to create greater customer delight?

The higher the degree of connection between your systems and resources and the customer, the greater the readiness of your organization.

Fire

It has been said that 'luck is the meeting of preparation and opportunity'. Thomas Jefferson claimed that he had been 'a very lucky man', but also noted how remarkable it was that the harder he worked, the 'luckier' he got. You cannot make yourself be lucky, but you can put yourself in positions where you are more likely to find opportunities. Having ensured your organizational readiness, go ahead and fire.

There is never the perfect moment. As Goethe wrote:[3]

Are you in earnest? Seize this very minute;
What you can do, or dream you can do, begin it;
Boldness has genius, power and magic in it.

New pathways open up when you stay in action. Opportunities arise when you are in communication with other people. Many entrepreneurs relate how one day they'll have a terrible meeting and feel like giving up. The next day they'll run into someone on the street who knows someone else who is exactly the person they needed in order to make all of their plans come together.

As Mark Fitzpatrick, who developed the popular First Watch software (later sold to Veritas Software), points out: 'You cannot make things follow a certain path, but if you stay active, you can do things to increase your chances of success. Your vision focuses you to be aware of opportunities and not filter them out. To succeed, you've got to take steps to improve yourself and keep looking for opportunities.'

When Jack Welch was reminiscing about his early days at GE, he said his one regret was that he didn't move faster. He moved much too fast for the taste of many GE people in the early 1980s, when he cut 130 000 jobs, and earned the nickname 'Neutron' Jack but, looking back, he felt that he had pulled his punches, and could have achieved more earlier.

When John Harvey-Jones was doing a similar turnaround job at the UK chemical company ICI, he said he was more interested in speed than in direction.

Both men saw time as the enemy, because they had to reshape, reinvent and reinvigorate their companies before they could start growing again. They felt they had to fire first and ask questions later. They knew there would be some collateral damage, but they saw it as the price they had to pay for getting back into growth mode again as quickly as possible.

Firing sooner rather than later is just as important when your organization is already alert, aligned and hungry, and you should always be on the look-out for ways to advance your ignition timing. Think about what it means to 'fire' in a new product or service development project. Does it simply mean completing the development process and launching the product or service, or could it mean something rather different, such as getting a new product out of the organization and into the hands of customers?

In the computer software industry it's called 'beta testing', and everyone does it. You get the new application up and running, but not yet finished (in the sense of being fully debugged and tested) and then give it to some carefully chosen customers. They try it out (in a real rather than a laboratory setting) knowing that it is work in progress. They see what it can do, find the bugs and other weaknesses, and then report back to you.

The relationship between a software supplier and its 'beta-testers' is highly specialized. The beta-testers are the firm's customers, in the sense that they are the sort of organizations that might buy the finished package, but they are also the firm's partners, in the sense that they are the penultimate step in the product development process. They help the supplier to get it right before the official launch.

Although the details of beta-test arrangements vary, it is clear that there is a mutually beneficial deal here. The beta-testers get to experiment with what might be competitively advantageous new technology earlier than their rivals, and the software supplier gets its new product tested, assessed and perhaps sold, before it is finished. Most important of all, beta-testing is an evidence procedure that reduces the risk of launching a new product that is riddled with bugs or that no one wants.

Could you devise a variant of the beta-test system in your business? If you supply complex, high-value products or services the answer is most probably 'yes', but even if you don't, it is worth thinking hard about how you could use selected customers as new product or service development partners on a long-term basis. Why not try to get customer feedback before launch? If you have got something they need, whether it is the basis of a brand new technology, the germ of a new service idea or the framework of a new product/service package, try to get it (warts and all, if need be) into their hands as soon as you can.

In exploring such possibilities, however, you should recognize that you may also be exploring different relationships with customers that could, if you press ahead with them, radically change your 'business model' and the shape and nature of your organization.

Aim: in-course correction

The new technology of guided weapons ushered in a different tactic based on feedback, rather than calibration. You didn't have to wait until you saw any part of your target. You could fire first and aim later, and pretty soon you had to because, if you spent time calibrating, you were dead.

A similar shift in tactics is occurring in business. It is being driven, in this case, not by any particular technology, but by the progressive removal of traditional market frictions in the form of time lags, transaction costs and imperfect information. The absence of friction speeds everything up and makes windows of opportunity far narrower. Your response, as leader, to the advent of frictionless business must be similar to the response of military strategists to the advent of guided weaponry. You should adopt a policy of acting right away, and devote a great deal of effort to the development and perfection of in-course correction systems.

Don Pickens says:

> If you get it wrong the first time, go back a second time, go back a third time. Lots of times you won't get it right until the third time. There's nothing wrong with that. The problem is, when you screw up the first time, a lot of people are telling you, 'You got it wrong, you should do something else'. The hard part is understanding what part of it you got right, and what you learned about what you got wrong.

We have seen how important it is for plans to be flexible and 'emergent', in the sense that they are constantly adapting to changing circumstances. In Chapter 1, we called this kind of adaptive planning 'skin-driven', because the messages that indicate the need for in-course corrections will come from your organization's customer-facing staff.

We also explained how carefully crafted 'operating mechanisms', such as the regional manager schedule Sam Walton, founder of Wal-Mart, devised for the company, can help to keep organizations in touch with their skin.

It is not a matter of abandoning your original plan and drafting and adopting a new one every time you receive new information. The challenge here is to make your original plan intrinsically provisional, in the same way that the initial course of a guided weapon is provisional. Guided weapons are always aimed in roughly the right direction, because you do not want them to waste too much time hunting, but they have an in-course aiming system that adapts their initial course to keep them on target.

The current course and the process for changing the current course comprise what mathematicians call a 'recursive function'. A function (or procedure, such as a plan) is 'recursive' when it 'calls' itself automatically as part of its own process.

A good example of recursiveness is Hofstadter's Law.[4] Promulgated nearly a quarter of a century ago by Douglas Hofstadter, it can still raise a smile. As well as illustrating the concept of recursion, it contains a strange wisdom that could be the mantra of this chapter.

Hofstadter's Law

Things always take longer than you expect, even when you take into account Hofstadter's Law.

The operating mechanisms (see Chapter 1) employed by Wal-Mart and other organizations to keep them in touch with their skin are themselves recursive functions. Think of it in terms of the distinction we made in Chapter 7 between being 'through time', and being 'in time'. If you are only 'through time', you focus on the goal, and you can only win or lose. In other words, you cannot see the trees for the wood. If you are only 'in time', you are so focused on the process, you forget the goal, and you can't see the wood for the trees.

To lead effectively in a business world in which you have to act before you know exactly where you are going, or how you will get there, you have to be both 'through time' and 'in time', at the same time. Aiming is no longer a simple calibration, after the completion of which you fire. It is a process that requires your constant attention.

But how is the strategy changed? What kind of systems do you need to assess course deviations, and make appropriate course corrections? Most systems fall into one of two basic types: 'periodic' systems, involving regular and frequent course-correction information gathering and interventions, and 'permanent' systems that can make corrections at any time.

Those Thursday morning meetings at Wal-Mart's Bentonville headquarters are examples of in-course correction systems that operate periodically. An example of a 'permanent', or 'always on' system was the set of 'key working assumptions' that was stuck up on the wall of the control room of Egg Bank, the UK financial services company launched by Prudential Assurance in 1998. The 'key working assumptions' comprised Egg's current strategy, but anyone involved in the project could change the assumptions at any time, simply by writing amendments on the list. This system meant Egg had very low inertia in the start-up phase, and could therefore change course extremely quickly. It needed to. When the interest rate Egg offered on its savings account led to a tidal wave of applications that overwhelmed its call centre, the young company metamorphosed from telephone bank to an Internet bank in just a few weeks.

Other examples of 'always on' systems are Jim Collins's 'catalytic mechanisms' that we referred to in Chapter 6.[5] Collins cites the example of Granite Rock in California, which sells gravel, concrete, sand and asphalt. In 1987 the family-owned business set out to become the Nordstrom of the aggregates market, and provide total customer satisfaction. It achieved its goal by adopting a policy it called 'short pay'. Customers are told at the bottom of every Granite Rock invoice that 'If you are not satisfied for any reason, don't pay us for it. Simply scratch out the line item, write a brief note about the problem, and return a copy of this invoice along with your check for the balance.'

As Collins points out, the system provides feedback about the quality of service, and puts considerable pressure on Granite Rock managers to find the causes of problems and solve them, to prevent repeated short payments.

Collins invented a catalytic mechanism for in-course correction for himself when he was teaching at Stanford. He was worried that his vocal students were drowning out their quieter, but more thoughtful classmates, so he gave everyone a red flag and told them they could wave it once each quarter, and that when they did, the rule was that everyone stopped talking and the floor was theirs.

The concept of in-course correction is at its most powerful at a deeply personal level, taking the results of our actions – both productive and unproductive – and using them as the basis for creating a better future.

Tools for thought

1. Organizational ready-fire-aim assessment

The questionnaire shown in Table 8.1 is divided into three sections: Ready, Fire and Aim. It is designed to assess the state of your organization in each of these areas, so that you can diagnose its capability and predict potential weaknesses.

In each section, score each item with 1 for low and 10 for high. Put your total score (out of a possible 100) at the end of each section. Compare the difference in score between sections to identify strengths and weaknesses. Plan remedial action to improve your lowest scoring section.

Table 8.1 *Organizational ready-fire-aim assessment*

Ready – be prepared										
Our purpose guides our day-to-day behaviour	1	2	3	4	5	6	7	8	9	10
The organization has a clear vision	1	2	3	4	5	6	7	8	9	10
All levels of management and staff understand and support the vision	1	2	3	4	5	6	7	8	9	10
The vision guides our day-to-day behaviour	1	2	3	4	5	6	7	8	9	10
The vision is supported by strategic objectives and implementation plan	1	2	3	4	5	6	7	8	9	10
The strategic objectives and implementation plan guide our day-to-day behaviour	1	2	3	4	5	6	7	8	9	10
I am personally aligned with the plan	1	2	3	4	5	6	7	8	9	10
My team has a visible stakeholder management plan to support the vision and visionary objectives	1	2	3	4	5	6	7	8	9	10
We have an organization alignment plan that supports the vision	1	2	3	4	5	6	7	8	9	10
The organization has a clear purpose	1	2	3	4	5	6	7	8	9	10
Total scores for Ready – be prepared										
Fire – act										
We are acting on the key issues facing us	1	2	3	4	5	6	7	8	9	10
The behaviour of all levels of management is driven on a day-to-day basis by the strategic plan	1	2	3	4	5	6	7	8	9	10
Each manager and member of staff knows their measures of success	1	2	3	4	5	6	7	8	9	10
The measures of success are visible on a day-by-day or week-by-week basis	1	2	3	4	5	6	7	8	9	10
Staff and junior managers feel they have the necessary authority to make a difference	1	2	3	4	5	6	7	8	9	10
Managers can respond to customer needs without going through major chains of decision making	1	2	3	4	5	6	7	8	9	10
There are only a small number of outstanding projects	1	2	3	4	5	6	7	8	9	10
Projects and goals get completed before new ones are initiated	1	2	3	4	5	6	7	8	9	10

Continued overleaf

Continued from previous page

Staff and managers go home at night feeling they have made a difference	1	2	3	4	5	6	7	8	9	10
Managers feel safe to 'act now and ask for forgiveness later'	1	2	3	4	5	6	7	8	9	10
Total scores for Fire – act										
Aim – in-course correction										
My team regularly has meetings to review our strategic plan against milestones	1	2	3	4	5	6	7	8	9	10
Milestones are measurable and give clear indications about whether we are on target or not	1 1	2 2	3 3	4 4	5 5	6 6	7 7	8 8	9 9	10 10
Each department and team regularly has meetings to check their goals against milestones and to review the relevance of goals	1	2	3	4	5	6	7	8	9	10
The strategic plan gets revisited at any point in the year if market, economic or technological circumstances change	1	2	3	4	5	6	7	8	9	10
Managers are not frightened of ending projects that are no longer relevant	1	2	3	4	5	6	7	8	9	10
The organizational culture lets managers cut programmes that have failed. Failure is accepted as a part of learning	1	2	3	4	5	6	7	8	9	10
Learnings are fed into future plans and initiatives	1	2	3	4	5	6	7	8	9	10
The organization is good at learning from past mistakes	1	2	3	4	5	6	7	8	9	10
People live the continuous improvement philosophy at all levels of management	1	2	3	4	5	6	7	8	9	10
The vision and the mission stay constant even though goals change according to circumstances	1	2	3	4	5	6	7	8	9	10
Total score for Aim – in-course correction										

2. Team ready-fire-aim assessment

In Chapters 5, 6 and 7 we introduced the thinking styles or metapro-grammes shown in Table 8.2.

Table 8.2 *Thinking styles revisited*

Thinking styles category	Dimensions	
Approach to goals	Towards the goal	Away from the problem
Locus of control	Proactive – 'self-referenced'	Reactive – 'other-referenced'
Approach to tasks	Options and choices	Following procedures
Time frame	Past-present-future	
Focus of interest	People Activities Places Things Information Time	
Point of view	Self—other—observer	
Mode of comparison	Similarity	Difference
Chunk size	Big chunk	Small chunk
Relationship to time	Through-time	In-time

We all know that planners and thinkers may not be so good at action, and that action-oriented people may not allow sufficient time to think and evaluate. However, the key to an effective ready-fire-aim approach is to ensure there is an appropriate balance of styles within your team.

The categorization of metaprogrammes shown in Table 8.3 indicates a bias towards 'ready' and 'aim' on one side, and 'fire' on the other. However, be warned: few people fit either profile exactly. Most people fall somewhere between the two extremes.

Table 8.3 *Ready-fire-aim profiles*

Thinking styles category	Ready and aim	Fire
Locus of control	Reactive – 'other-referenced'	Proactive – 'self-referenced'
Time frame	Past to future	Present
Relationship to time	Through time	In time
Focus of interest	Time – information	Activities
Chunk size	Small chunk	Big chunk
Point of view	Observer	Self

In order to evaluate your team, make some estimates about your team in terms of these styles as shown in Table 8.4. (Need we say that your estimates will need in-course correction over time as you continue to compare your assessment of people's thinking style with their actual behaviour?) People can score on both the 'ready' and the 'act' list; for example, someone may be equally likely to adopt observer and self points of view.

Table 8.4   *Team ready-fire-aim assessment*

Thinking styles	Person							
	I	2	3	4	5	6	7	8
Ready aim tendencies								
Reactive locus of control:								
Time frame:								
Past-future								
Time: *Through time*								
Focus of interest: *Information Time*								
Point of view: *Observer*								
Chunk size: *Small chunk*								
Number of 'Ready' styles								
Fire tendencies								
Locus of control: *Proactive*								
Time frame: *Present*								
Time: *In-time*								
Focus of interest: *Activities*								
Point of view: *Self*								
Chunk size: *Big chunk*								
Number of Fire styles								

Total the scores and review the composition of your team in the light of these assessments. Decide how to compensate for any imbalances, either by changing the team composition or by 'buddying' within the team.

3. In-course correction: the power of visible messaging

One way to improve in-course correction in a business is to create visible measures of your goals, so that as many people as possible can see whether the business is on track or not.

Some call centres have visible messaging showing the number of calls picked up within an acceptable time frame. At various strategic points, including the staff entrance and the visitor's entrance, a sign shows either a red stop light or a green go light. Red means off target, green means the target has been achieved. Information from the previous day's calls are analysed overnight and displayed to produce in-course correction in the organization's performance the following day.

1. List some key measures for your business or division.
2. Select from the list a measure that is sufficiently sensitive that it would provide relevant feedback to staff and managers if it were supplied on a daily or weekly basis.
3. Find a graphic, auditory (using sounds or music) or kinesthetic (something that gives a feeling) form as the vehicle for expressing on target or off target results.
4. Test the idea on some colleagues, making sure to mix rogue monkeys as well as more conservative influences in your focus group.
5. Act: implement the visible message of a performance measure.
6. In-course correction: after a period of operation, review and improve your messaging.

For more resources on ready, fire, aim, see www.AlphaLeaders.com

Conclusion

Ready-fire-aim is the reality for organizations struggling to keep up with the speed of change in their markets. Time spent calibrating before trying something out is often time – and opportunity – wasted.

Partnerships with lead customers are key to an effective ready-fire-aim strategy, but may require a fundamental rethink of the shape and nature of your organization.

The boldness of action has its reward. If you seek genius, power and magic, as Goethe said, begin it now.

In the following chapter, we address the persistence required to make action effective.

References

1. Interview by Dilts Strategy Group.
2. *Ibid.*

3. Attributed to John Anster 'in a very free translation' of *Faust* in 1835.
4. Attributed to Douglas Hofstadter.
5. Collins, J. (1999) Turning goals into results: the power of catalytic mechanisms, *Harvard Business Review*, July–August.

9

Dogged Pursuit (and Knowing When to Stop)

If at first you don't succeed, try again. Then quit. No use being a damn fool about it.

W.C. Fields

Climbing the bell towers of The Temple of the Sagrada Familia in Barcelona, you arrive at a bridge suspended in mid-air between two enormous spires. They look like no other cathedral spires in the world, seeming more like organic growths emerging from the ground than man-made structures. Vibrant mosaics spiral around them, inscribing the words Sanctus! Sanctus! Sanctus! (Holy! Holy! Holy!).

The spires are at one end of a vast, half-built structure. At the other end are further spires, turrets and domes. Some of the spires seem to be draped with giant oranges, like Christmas baubles, clustered at their peaks. Facing out from the main building is an enormous pedestal shaped like a Christmas tree, with carved doves roosting in it, and at the top a goddess who looks more like a great Tibetan or Hindu deity than the Virgin Mary. Unrelated systems of sensuous curving design are juxtaposed in what architects call a 'warped' form of Gothic architecture.

Anton Gaudi's masterpiece is still under construction, 120 years after it was first started in 1881. Gaudi worked intermittently on the project until he died in 1926. Other architects took over the work, which was interrupted during the Spanish Civil War and the Second World War, when the building was seriously damaged.

This cathedral was Gaudi's prayer to God, and an expression of his confidence in the enduring values embodied in it. Just before the Spanish Civil War, Joan Maragall, the Catalan poet prophesied:[1]

Amidst misery and rage and smoke,
The temple . . . rises and prospers
Awaiting a faithful yet to come.

Construction continues to this day. It is hoped that this great monument will be completed some time in the first half of the 21st century. There are numerous clubs and organizations fund-raising for its completion.

As time goes on, Gaudi's vision has become more and more inspiring. When finished, Sagrada Familia will have taken more than 150 years to build, and will probably be the last great cathedral ever constructed, in an effort reaching from the 19th to the 21st century.

Gaudi relentlessly pursued his vision, sleeping in his workshop for the last eight years of his life rather than give up his dream. After his death, his vision lived on. Other architects picked up the challenge, adopting his vision and pursuing his dream, despite physical and financial hardship.

Gaudi's dogged persistence in building a physical structure that defies architectural convention has touched thousands of people. People living in Barcelona have been so inspired by Gaudi that the Roman Catholic Church has started the process of beatification, to make him Saint Anton. Already, people light candles at Gaudi's tomb and pray there.

Gaudi's story symbolizes the virtues of patience and perseverance. We believe they are great virtues in business as well as ambitious architectural projects. Research by A. T. Kearney on Top Performing Companies (companies that exceeded their expected return on equity over a 15-year period) found that the most highly correlated factor among the strongest performers was the longevity of the CEO. It seems that continuity in direction and leadership is critical to success over a sustained period.

But it is a small step from the virtues of patience and perseverance to the vice of an obsessive commitment to a hopeless quest. You also need to know when to stop. No goal is worth an infinite amount of time, money, blood and sweat. Persevere but, as W. C. Fields said, beware of 'being a damn fool about it'.

Dogged pursuit

In his book, *Managing on the Edge*, Richard Pascale illustrates his research on changing fashions in management techniques in a graphic called the 'Ebbs, Flows, and Residual Impact of Business Fads, 1950–1988'.[2] A business 'fad' is an idea that gets a lot of managers excited for a while, inspires a lot of action and is then quietly forgotten as newer ideas claim the attention of managers. But the 'faddishness', or otherwise, of an idea depends far less on its intrinsic merits than on the durability of its influence. W. Edwards Deming, the originator of total quality management, put forward ideas about statistical quality control that have had a profound and enduring effect on Japanese businesses, but according to Pascale, 75% of the 'quality circles' they inspired in America in the early 1980s had been abandoned by 1986.

In some cases, of course, management ideas become less topical, not because managers lose interest in them, but because they are so widely adopted that they cease to offer competitive advantage. Although 'quality circles' never really caught on in the United States, the idea of quality as a differentiator did; so much so indeed that through an explosion of Total Quality Management (TQM) programmes in the late 1980s, it became a commodity. This is often the way. An idea that begins as a 'differentiation' criterion is so widely emulated it becomes a 'qualification' criterion – a minimum standard firms have to meet just to become contenders in their marketplaces.

More often, however, good ideas become fads in retrospect because they are not pursued with enough determination and patience. They are launched with fanfares, workshops, 'townhall' meetings, wall charts and other oral and written exhortations but the energy is not maintained, and other fads soon replace them.

A vision and values exercise recently conducted by a global financial services organization provides a typical example of this lack of determination. The top management was aware that the old vision was not sufficiently inspirational, and wanted to clarify, articulate and align behind a refocused purpose. Interviews with a vertical cross-section of senior managers produced a powerful new vision statement, and an explicit set of company values. Considerable investment was made in marketing the new vision and values both internally and externally. Twenty thousand employees attended facilitated discussion groups carefully designed to give each person a chance to explore his or her own personal relationship with the vision and values.

Despite this considerable investment, it is unlikely that the organization will ever embody either the proposed vision or the values. For example, one of the values is 'teamwork', but the senior management of the firm has a consistent track record of poor teamworking. A half-day values exercise cannot possibly change this. To implement the vision requires a high degree of pain and dogged persistence on the part of management, particularly if managers are to embody the values in their own behaviour. A three-year, multiactivity change programme would be a more appropriate level of effort for genuine culture change to occur.

Setting goals with insufficient effort to achieve them has two effects: first it robs the current idea of any chance to prove its worth, and second it instills the belief in employees that there's no need to take notice of any new initiative because their leader's mercurial attention will have shifted to a new fad within a few months anyway. Employees know they will never be called to account for their failure to comply with the current initiative.

It boils down to a matter of perceived commitment and conviction. If people believe you are committed to an idea or course of action, and that you are convinced it will improve the organization's performance, they will take it seriously and align themselves with it. The idea has to be big, however, in the sense that it clearly offers substantial benefits, and you have to keep plugging away at it, until people act on it without thinking.

Gaudi's dream of a cathedral that broke all the rules was big enough, but it would not have become a way of life for his successors had he not pursued it with perseverance and conviction. Stretch goals are not achieved by the dreams of leaders alone, but by beliefs that become so deeply embedded in the minds of large numbers of people that they pursue those beliefs without thinking about it.

Organizations have conscious and unconscious 'minds' that are constantly interacting in an endless cycle of creation and destruction. They could not operate without vast portfolios of codified knowledge that enable them to act without thinking, and they could not respond flexibly to new situations without conscious minds that are constantly scanning their environments and refreshing their codified portfolios in the light of what they learn.

Golfers trying to change their swings know how vulnerable their unconscious knowledge is to conscious scrutiny. As David Hurst has pointed out, golf swings are like organizations, in that both consist of hierarchies of processes, the stability of which is achieved, at each level, by feedback loops. Stability emerges when the big, slow processes constrain the smaller, faster ones.[3]

The hierarchical, systemic nature of business organizations – and golf swings – precludes the quick fix, because changes in the big, slow processes cascade up through the smaller, faster ones. A change in grip, for example, demands a series of adjustments to legs, hips, shoulders, arms and hands. In other words, actual (as opposed to ideal) swings consist of systems of offsetting errors. When one is corrected, other features that were compensating for it become new errors.

It is the same with organizations. You cannot simply abandon old habits and adopt new ones – the compensating habits have been too well learned and are too deeply embedded in the unconscious.

The solution is to abandon the search for the quick fix, accept the complex nature of tacit knowledge, and work on one level at a time, beginning with the big, slow processes. Things may get worse, for a while, as compensating processes higher up are rendered counter-productive by lower level changes, but this must be lived with. If the focus is on immediate results, the mind will tend to default to old, familiar actions, and embed errors more deeply still.

If you want to transform your organization, you should act like a golf swing doctor. Patience and doggedness are essential. You must identify errors in tacit knowledge, summon them up, deepest first, to consciousness, fix them, 'drill' people in the new activities, and then let them sink down again to where they can work automatically, without conscious thought.

Mr Miyaki, the hero's *sensei* in the film *Karate Kid*, drilled his student in the basic arm movements of the martial art by asking him to spend hours painting a fence in a carefully prescribed way. Drilling takes time and ties up resources, but it is the only way to get beliefs and practices 'in the muscle', where they can drive action without thought.

The patience and perseverance needed to embed new beliefs and reflexes in a group of people will not seem to them, or to their leader, to be worth the time and effort they require without a clear and compelling goal. The Karate Kid was bored and frustrated painting his teacher's fence until he realized it had been a drill to embed the reflexes in his unconscious mind that he would need to achieve his goal of becoming adept at karate. People will not tolerate the frustrations of the endless drills required to improve their golf swings unless they set a high value on the outcome.

The leader's job is to spell out long-term goals that make tolerable what would otherwise be seen as the boring pursuit of a series of apparently trivial, constantly changing subgoals. Leaders with the mental agility and patience needed to try different approaches when progress stalls, or make in-course corrections when circumstances dictate, must keep an overall vision in the mind of the organization.

Fads and contingencies may come and go, but visions must endure. When President John F. Kennedy promised, in 1961, that 'before this decade is out' America would send a man to the Moon and return him safely to earth, he set a deadline for a clear goal, compelling enough to transcend any possible frustrations, failures and set-backs that people involved in the project might encounter on the way. And, by staking his own and his country's reputation on meeting the deadline (which, in the event, was reached with 18 months to spare), he was committing unlimited resources to the goal. Articulating a compelling vision, and sticking with it through thick and thin, is a core skill of the Alpha leader.

The dogged pursuer

Robert the Bruce was born in 1274, a distant heir to the Scottish throne. His grandfather claimed the throne when it fell vacant in 1290, but Bruce paid homage to King Edward I of England, after Edward refused to acknowledge another king of Scotland.

After the defeat of the Scottish patriot William Wallace (played by Mel Gibson in the film *Braveheart*) at Falkirk in 1299, Edward I appointed the apparently compliant Bruce as one of four regents to rule Scotland, and he was among those Edward consulted before he proclaimed Scotland a 'province' of England in 1305.

However, Bruce was not quite the sycophantic local nobleman Edward I took him to be. In the rebellions against English rule from 1295 to 1304, he is believed to have been among Wallace's leading supporters and was cer-tainly implicated in the murder of John 'the Red' Comyn, who had a claim on the Scottish crown, in a church at Dumfries on 10 February 1306. Bruce immediately proclaimed his right to the throne, and on 27 March 1306, was crowned King Robert I.

It was not a peaceful accession, however. English garrisons held many of the important castles in Scotland; Edward regarded his erstwhile puppet as a traitor, and set out to crush him. Robert I was defeated in battle twice in 1306. His wife and many of his supporters were imprisoned, three of his brothers were executed and Bruce himself became a fugitive, his estates were confiscated, and he and his followers were excommunicated.

It was while in exile on a remote island off the west coast of Scotland that Bruce – defeated, destitute, in mourning for three of his brothers and anxious about the fates of his wife and friends – is said to have been inspired by the endeavours of a spider. Legend has it that, as he sat hiding in a dank, freezing cave, he became mesmerized by the work of a spider building its web. As he watched, he saw that each time the spider managed to secure its web, sudden gusts of wind in the cave mouth broke its threads. Undeterred, the spider kept mending the web. Time and again the delicate threads broke, and time and again the spider mended them, until at last the web was finished.

Seeing this tiny creature's determination to succeed despite repeated setbacks, Bruce became determined to persevere in his struggle. After his return to Ayrshire in February 1307, Bruce patiently attracted supporters to his cause, and slowly built up his strength.

Within two years, Bruce's forces captured Galloway, Douglasdale, the forest of Selkirk and most of the eastern borders. In 1313 Robert himself defeated John Comyn, the Earl of Buchan (a cousin of John 'the Red'), and took Perth from an English garrison. His supporters captured Edinburgh in early 1314, and on 24 June of that year, they defeated the English army sent to relieve the garrison of Stirling at the decisive battle of Bannockburn.

Hostilities continued, and Robert invaded England on two occasions before a truce was signed with Edward II in 1323. Finally, in 1328, a treaty was signed which recognized Scotland's independence and the right of Bruce to the throne. The web was finally finished.

An unexpected footnote to this story was the crowning, in 1603, of one of Bruce's descendants as James I of England. Robert the Bruce could never have dreamed when he was watching the spider that returning to action, and pursuing his goals, would lead to the foundation of the United Kingdom under a *Scottish* king.

The leader capable of dogged pursuit has very distinctive characteristics. In addition to patience and tenacity, leaders must cultivate other personal qualities that may not be part of their natures: skins thick enough to cope with personal attacks without getting disheartened, but sensitive enough to detect weak signals; the mental agility to find alternative routes through an apparently impenetrable obstacle; and the resilience needed to retain their self-esteem after personal failures.

Walt Disney was fired from his first job, because he 'lacked imagination'; Michael Jordan was dropped from his high school's basketball team; Richard Branson was expelled from school; the Beatles were turned down by Decca, the first recording company they approached. Such failures can become assets, because people remember them and see them as evidence of strength of character and of a determination to win against all odds.

On a more prosaic level, the selling skills needed to get visions and goals into the muscles of your followers are exemplified by the qualities needed in 'cold-calling'. It is always a frustrating and sometimes an ego-bruising way to sell, because, however carefully you construct your list, most of the people you call will not feel the need for what you have to offer or be in the mood to be persuaded. Some will be so involved in a task they will find your call extremely irritating. As a 'system', however, cold-calling can be very effective. Some people actually enjoy it, because they have learned to see each rejection as part of the price they pay for the tiny percentage of calls that are productive and as a contribution to their understanding of the marketplace.

Cold-callers of this kind treat failure as feedback, in the same way as the inventors we discussed in Chapter 2. They are constantly experimenting with new approaches and arguments, different tones of voice, variations in style and timing, and other variables. They search their results avidly for clues about how to refine their methods, and after a while the best approaches to the kind of respondents they are calling at a particular time come to their lips, unbidden. They are flexible but determined, as leaders must be when doggedly pursuing their goals.

The act of stopping

A tourist in Guatemala was puzzled when she stumbled across the chapel of a local cult containing the effigy of a strange deity. Although the devotees were brown-eyed, dark-skinned Indians, the smiling statue had blue eyes and white skin, and was surrounded by bottles of alcohol and paper money.

'What,' the tourist wondered, 'is all this about?'

It transpired that the deity's name was Maximon, but he was better known to the tourist as Judas Iscariot. The reason for Maximon's deification was easily explained and perfectly logical. The Indians worshipped Maximon/Judas, because he was the only character in the scriptures of Catholicism, the religion that had expelled the gods of their ancestors, who had got the better of Jesus. The alcohol symbolized the last supper, and the money symbolized the 30 pieces of silver Judas was paid to betray Christ.

The Guatemalan population is predominantly Roman Catholic, but it is an odd kind of convert to Christianity who worships Judas for betraying Jesus. The old gods are long gone, but the profound resentment the Indians felt at the expulsion lives on in Maximon. They were converted officially, but at heart they remained pagan, with the new beliefs simply overlaid on their traditional customs and religion.

The same thing happens in companies. People get converted officially to new strategies and programmes, but the old ones often live on because no one has stopped them. A hospital reengineering programme aimed at cutting cycle time by 40% was well into its stride when it was discovered that an older quality circle programme, aimed at a more modest 2% cycle time reduction, was still running. Like laws and religions, old change programmes seldom die, they just fade away into the background, and the only overt sign of their survival is their drag on new initiatives.

As the economist, John Maynard Keynes, once pointed out: 'the greatest difficulty lies not in persuading people to accept new ideas, but in persuading them to abandon old ones.'[4]

Here is the essential paradox of dogged pursuit: while it is critical to pursue a goal relentlessly, it is also important to have the sensitivity to realize when to stop.

Microsoft's appeal to the Supreme Court against a ruling that it had abused its monopoly provides a useful example of the skill of stopping. The Supreme Court declined to take the case and it seemed unlikely that, if the trust-busters tried to stop the launch of the company's new Windows XP operating system, the judge appointed to decide on remedies for Microsoft's illegal behaviour would have time to issue an injunction. It had long been clear, however, that the company was embroiled in litigation on a long-term basis, and would be spending a lot of management time on defending its position and a lot of money on lawyers for years to come.

'Rule number one at Microsoft,' the *Economist* declaimed, 'is never give up,'[5] and for Bill Gates *aficionados*, it was not hard to see the company's founder as a latter-day Robert the Bruce, patiently struggling for the freedom to run his company as he saw fit, against a spiteful antitrust bureaucracy bent on hobbling the preeminent symbol of America's victorious assault on the world software market.

Others were suggesting, however, that it was time for Microsoft to yield to the legal onslaught, reach a reasonable settlement on remedies and re-focus its energies on its business. They argued that the company's dogged defence of practices the court had adjudged illegal was damaging its reputation and creating new threats. The US Senate had planned hearings on Windows XP, the press comment was becoming increasingly hostile – the *San Jose Mercury*, for instance, had launched a 'Freedom from Microsoft' campaign – and Linux, the free, 'open source' PC operating system that Microsoft itself regarded as a potentially powerful competitor to Windows, was waiting in the wings, ready to pick up the pieces.

The *Economist* advised Microsoft to delay the launch of Windows XP until the legality of the new software had been established in the courts. 'The firm could thus demonstrate to the world,' the influential weekly argued, 'that it is not always bent on pushing things to the limit, and rebuild the trust it has lost. Alas, given Microsoft's DNA, such a move looks likely to remain wishful thinking. More's the pity. Tenacity might be a must in the software world, but in politics it is often a recipe for disaster.'[6]

It was up to Gates to decide whether to stop, and it was a tougher deci-sion than the *Economist* implied. He had to take into account not just the costs (in legal fees, top management time and damage to the firm's reputa-tion) of continuing, but also the costs of stopping. In addition to the costs of the remedies agreed with the court, the 'intangible' costs of stopping could be considerable if 'we never give up' really is an integral part of the firm's culture. Giving up takes courage, if it can be seen by your followers as an act of cowardice.

Like compensating errors in golf swings, out-of-date goals and processes need to be called up into the organization's conscious mind, tested for valid-ity and, if they fail, given the last rites. Without periodic flushing out, oper-ating mechanisms, beliefs and habits overlay each other and create complex, stratified cultures that become progressively less manageable. Clearing out such cultural clutter can liberate resources that can be put to better use elsewhere, and can make your organization more adaptable.

The need to make exits from programmes as well as enter them highlights the importance of exit costs. Everyone knows about 'barriers to entry' into industries or markets, but there are also 'barriers to exit' and you must try to minimize them in advance. We have discussed the cultural costs Microsoft might incur if it abandons its legal struggle, but there are many other kinds of exit costs that are easier to judge. A major car manufacturer had begun a $6 million, '6Sigma' cost reduction programme, when it found a better programme that cost $3 million. Despite this opportunity, the company stuck with the original programme because it would have had to pay a $1.5 million penalty for pulling out early.

Sign no such clauses. Look before you leap. Act like a burglar and secure your escape route before entering.

Tools for thought

1. Imagineering

It was once said of Walt Disney: 'there were actually three different Walts: the *dreamer*, the *realist*, and the *spoiler*. You never knew which one was coming to your meeting.' This is not only an insight into Disney, but also into the process of creativity and problem solving – a process that Disney called 'imagineering'. Imagineering involves the coordination of three subprocesses: Dreamer, Realist and Critic, all of which are necessary to bring dreams to life.[7]

In this chapter, we are particularly interested in two things: the dogged pursuit of a vision that is worth manifesting, and knowing when to stop if persistence has turned into rigidity and sheer bloodymindedness. We advocate dogged persistence around a core and unchanging purpose, combined with weak signals detection and the mental agility to reshape the means of achieving your goals as necessary.

The following tool uses the Dreamer, Realist, Critic model to help you clarify your vision and test it for its robustness, so you can be confident in your dogged pursuit.

A Dreamer without a Realist cannot turn ideas into tangible expressions. A Critic and a Dreamer without a Realist just become stuck in a perpetual conflict. A Dreamer and a Realist might create things, but they might not be very good ideas without a Critic. The Critic helps to evaluate and refine the products of creativity (when destructive, a Critic is a 'spoiler'; when constructive, a Critic is an 'adviser' or 'editor').

The Dreamer is necessary in order to form new ideas and goals, generating alternatives and possibilities. The Realist is necessary as a means to

transform ideas into concrete expressions and actions. The Critic is necessary as a filter for refining ideas and avoiding possible problems, evaluating
pay-offs and drawbacks.

Disney's creative process can also be applied to groups and teams. The
creative cycle of a group or team often involves the natural movement
between Dreamer (the big picture or 'vision'), Realist (the establishment of
microobjectives to reach the larger goal), and Critic (the search for missing
links and potential problems).

Balance is considered by many leaders as the key to managing a group's
creative process. In order to solve a problem or produce a plan effectively,
no one stage or thinking style can be favoured at the expense of the others.
For effective group problem solving, it is important to incorporate all
three of the stages of the creative cycle (Dreamer, Realist, Critic) and the
different points of view of group members in all three stages.

Disney, for example, had different rooms for the Dreamer, Realist and
Critic. He had one room that was a Dreamer room, with pictures and inspirational drawings and sayings all over the walls. Everything was chaotic and
colourful in this room, and criticisms were not allowed – only dreams. For
their Realist space, the animators had their own drawing tables, stocked
with all kinds of equipment, tools and instruments that they would need to
manifest the dreams. The tables were arranged in a large room in which all
of the animators could see and talk to each other. For the Critic's space,
Disney had a little room that was underneath the stairs where they would
look at the prototype pencil sketches and evaluate them. The room always
seemed cramped and hot, so they called it the 'sweatbox'.

The following exercise directs the process of a group through the stages
of Dreamer, Realist and Critic by answering and exploring a range of
questions appropriate for each phase.

1.   Design a process that clearly has three phases or sessions: Dreamer,
     Realist and Critic. For example, you could plan three hours with an
     hour for each phase, or three two-hour sessions, or for something more
     important, a series of meetings to create the vision, some sessions to
     plan, and an evaluation process at the end to test the plan.
     (a) Think about how to create the right atmosphere for each stage. For
          example, use an off-site conference room at a comfortable venue
          with no tables and lots of flip charts and coloured pens for the

Dreamer stage. The Realist phase can be done in your standard project-planning environment. For the Critic phase, think about the circumstances in which your organization best expresses constructive criticism and challenge in a way that is both safe for the challenger and heard by the receivers. Seek to emulate this environment.

(b) Make sure that the participants you invite
   i. are sufficiently diverse;
   ii. cover all the views you want to incorporate;
   iii. have a good balance of natural Dreamers, Realists and Critics; that is to say, ideas people, planners and conservative types.

(c) Plan how the process cycles back after the Critic stage: what do you do with the 'blockers' that the Critic phase comes up with? How do you take these back into the planning cycle?

(d) Ask yourself how you will know that the Dreamer-Realist-Critic cycle is complete? Will you want the whole group to agree, or are they simply being consulted in a decision making process that is ultimately yours?

2. Explain the model to the group, and agree on some ground rules that support the thinking style for each phase or session. For example
   (a) Dreamer:
      i. any idea is a good idea;
      ii. wild and wacky ideas are good;
      iii. no idea is too big;
      iv. no criticism of individuals or their ideas;
      v. build on other people's ideas.
   (b) Realist
      i. use our best business planning and project planning skills;
      ii. if it's a stretch goal, let's put aside our concern about feasibility and buy-in from others, and plan before we evaluate;
      iii. no criticism of the scale of the project until we have worked it through;
      iv. we will adopt a 'can-do' attitude.
   (c) Critic
      i. let's be tough but kind (disagree without being disagreeable);
      ii. let's criticize the project not the planners;

    iii. look after the people engaged in this process while speaking our mind about the project;

    iv. we can challenge the boss' ideas safely;

    v. worst-case thinking is good. Let's be cautious.

3. Run the process.
4. Review process.
   (a) What worked well?
   (b) What did not work well?
   (c) What would you do differently next time?

Use the following questions as prompts for discussion in each phase.

Questions for the Dreamer Phase

- Create the vision and establish the pay-offs.
  - Why are you doing this?
  - What is the purpose?
  - What are the pay-offs?
  - What will happen if you achieve this? What possibilities do you see?
  - How will you know that you have achieved it?
  - When can you expect to achieve it?
  - Where do you want to be in the future?
  - Who do you want to be or be like?
  - If there were no constraints, what could you accomplish?

Questions for the Realist Phase

- State the specific goal in positive terms.
- Establish time frames and milestones for progress.
- Make sure it can be initiated and maintained by the appropriate person or group and that progress is measurable.
  - What will you be doing?
  - How specifically will the idea be implemented?
  - How will the performance criteria be tested?
  - Who will do it? (Assign responsibility and secure commitment.)
  - When will each phase be implemented?
  - When will the overall goal be completed?
  - Where will each phase be carried out?
  - Why is each step necessary?

Questions for the Critic Phase

- Establish the disadvantages and how to ameliorate them.
    - Why might someone object to this new idea?
    - Who will this new idea affect, and who will make or break the effectiveness of the idea? What are their needs and pay-offs?
    - What positive things do you get out of your current way(s) of doing things?
    - How can you keep those things when you implement the new idea?
    - When and where would you not want to implement this new idea?
- Assess and counter the risks.
    - What are the risks?
        - Financial?
        - In terms of the credibility of individuals or department or organization?
    - What is the worst-case scenario?
        - What are the financial implications?
        - What are the personal or organizational implications?
    - What can you do to make the risks acceptable? (Use the chunking down exercise from Chapter 2.)
- Evaluate the project compared to other potential projects.
    - Does this project fulfil your 80:20 criteria? (See Chapter 7.)
    - Does it really fulfil your vision?
    - Is it the best use of your resources? Could the same resource applied to another project have a greater impact on your chosen mission or vision?
    - Does it really support your key business objectives?

It is worth noting that Critics are often considered the most difficult people to handle in an interaction because of their seemingly negative focus. The most challenging problems occur when the Critic doesn't just criticize the dream or the plan, but begins to criticize the Dreamer and Realist. It is different to say, 'That idea is stupid,' than to say, 'You are stupid for having that idea.'

It is important to keep in mind that criticism, like all other behaviour, is positively intended (see Chapter 5 for more on positive intention). The two most effective principles for dealing with a Critic are to find the positive purpose behind the criticism, and to turn criticisms into questions.

The following sequence is a practical strategy to turn a criticism into a question. Ask the Critic:

1. 'What is your objection to the solution or the plan?'
2. 'What is the positive intention behind the criticism?'
3. 'Given your intention, what is the question that you have about the solution or plan? If you have a concern about implementation, ask "How would you . . .?" '

2. Prioritizing initiatives

Kicking off a new initiative can be fun, high energy and very motivating. It can also be met with a groan of exhaustion and disbelief from an organization overwhelmed with 'flavour of the month' change programmes and struggling under the weight of initiative fatigue.

An organization's existing initiatives are rarely scrutinized to see where projects can be stopped, reoriented or merged into a new programme. More often, the new programmes are simply left to run alongside existing ones, adding layer upon layer of projects until the organization's change programme starts to resemble geological strata.

It can be hard to identify which projects to eliminate and which to refocus. The matrix in Figure 9.1 provides an approach to assessing current projects with a view to stopping lower value initiatives, and reassigning resources to higher value ones.

Start by taking an inventory of on-going initiatives. Divide them into an A, B, C list based on the amount of resource they are consuming and the size of their anticipated benefit.

There will probably be a myriad smaller projects that could take months to document. The 80:20 law operates here – focus on the 20% of projects that consume 80% of the resources.

Take the A list of projects and, for each project, document the following:

●   the benefit expected (high, medium, low);
●   the period in which the benefit can be achieved (short, medium or long term);
●   the feasibility of implementation (high, medium, low);
●   the investment required to achieve the benefits (£).

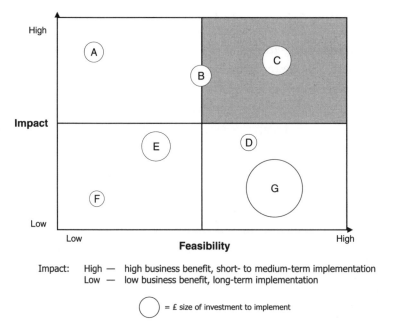

Figure 9.1   Prioritizing initiatives

Map each project on the matrix shown in Figure 9.1. Combine the benefit and time period into one average high, medium, low rating for each project. Use the size of investment required to deliver the benefits as the size of the bubble denoting each project.

Do the same on separate matrices for B and C projects. Then working with a multidisciplinary team, work out a strategy for each project:

- eliminate;
- refocus;
- merge;
- refresh/add resource.

Track each project over time to make sure that these strategies are implemented. Old projects sometimes take a long time to die out and can resurface in different guises. Make process or policy changes as necessary. For example, if a project scheduled to be eliminated has a charge code associated with it, ensure the charge code is closed and finance/accounts know that they should reject any time or expense charged to that code after the project is shut down.

3. Connecting initiatives to business outcomes

A retailer was experiencing severe revenue pressure and starting to lose market share. The brand remained relatively strong, but it appeared that shoppers were spending less on each visit, and also were visiting stores less frequently. A number of cost measures had been undertaken to address cost competitiveness, and major product lines were being redesigned. However, when each initiative was mapped against the retailer's turnaround strategy, it became clear that in the critical area of increasing footfall in stores, no initiative was in place.

This is a common finding when working with complex organizations. As part of the annual budgeting process for a government department, a similar exercise was undertaken. Despite launching a large number of initiatives during the preceding year, not one of them impacted the department's primary goal.

The following tool has proved useful in reconnecting an organization's change initiatives to its overall business goals. We typically see that there is a missing link: companies are usually clear on their goals, and pretty clear on their main change initiatives, but it is often hard to see where they connect with each other, and even harder to detect whether the business critical areas are adequately addressed.

The simple framework shown in Figure 9.2 can be helpful in making the right connections and identifying where initiatives should be prioritized or eliminated.

Start by documenting the organization or department's goal. Make it as clear and actionable as possible. Then identify what the organization will need to do well in order to achieve this goal. For example, for a hospital whose goal was to become the leading teaching and research hospital in the United Kingdom, one key 'do well' was to ensure clinical excellence and outcome-based treatment. Try to limit the 'do wells' to a maximum of five to seven main areas.

Next identify two or three key measures against each 'do well'. In the example above, outcome-based treatment was measured through the percentage of clinical interventions that were research based.

Against each key measure, map existing change initiatives that are designed to improve that measure.

Take a look at the mapping. Is there an overload of initiatives against one area of 'do wells'? Is there a gap against any key measure?

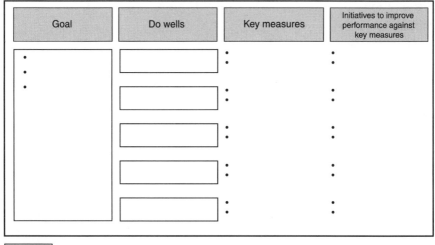

Goal	Do wells	Key measures	Initiatives to improve performance against key measures
•		•	•
•		•	•
•		•	•
		•	•
		•	•
		•	•
		•	•
		•	•
		•	•
		•	•

Example

• The manufacturing leadership team adds value by building and refining strategies, providing resources, prioritizing and ensuring completion of critical tasks so that customers' needs are met	• Marketing excellence: Be the recognized market leader through the superior way we anticipate the needs of our customers and channel partners, communicate the value of our products and services, and provide user-friendly support	• Market share • Schedule attainment • Manufacturing customer contacts	• Identify and eliminate customer dissatisfiers • Work closely with BUs to drive supply chain excellence

Figure 9.2 *Connecting initiatives to business goals*

Identify steps to fill gaps, and reduce or eliminate projects in areas of overload.

Reassess the situation regularly as business requirements change. Use this map to assess each new initiative prior to launch.

For more resources on dogged pursuit, go to www.AlphaLeaders.com

Conclusion

High performance organizations stick at things. Their leaders display dogged pursuit in the attainment of core goals, maintaining perseverance and constancy of purpose over long periods of time. This energy and commitment has ripple effects throughout the organization, converting 'faddishness' into a long-term dedication to the achievement of strongly held goals.

Dogged pursuit also requires leaders to acknowledge where particular routes to a goal are blocked, and where certain initiatives could be more profitably directed. In other words, they pay attention to where the organization should stop, rather than focusing exclusively on where it should start afresh.

The following chapter pulls together all three Alpha Leadership themes, and ends with a call to action for leaders everywhere.

References

1. Maragall, J. (1993) Oda Nueva a Barcelona, in *Poesia*, Planeta.
2. Pascale, R. (1991) *Managing on the Edge: How the Smartest Companies Use Conflict to Stay Ahead*, Simon & Schuster.
3. Hurst, D. (n.d.) *Golf and Management: A Complex Symmetry*, www.speakers.co.uk/books/davhurpr1.htm.
4. Attributed to John Maynard Keynes, http://www.brint.com/books/excerpts/delphi.htm.
5. The *Economist* (2001) Nothing if not tenacious, 11 August.
6. *Ibid*.
7. Dilts, R. (1994) *Strategies of Genius, Volume I*, Meta Publications. There is also a software program that takes individuals and groups through the Imagineering process, available from Journey to Genius at www.journeytogenius.com

10

Conclusion

Après nous le déluge.

Madame de Pompadour

All three authors have, by different routes, invented, discovered or stumbled upon the approaches, perspectives and tools of *Alpha Leadership* set out in the previous chapters, because, without knowing it at first, we were all looking for them.

Our individual quests, which led first to friendships and then to collaboration on this book, were inspired by the time we spent with our clients, helping leaders to be successful in today's demanding workplace.

Why are people so stressed? How come people work all hours and still wonder, late at night or at moments of reflection, whether all the effort is worth while? 'What can be done about it?' we asked ourselves and each other. 'What practical perspective and tools can we find, develop and describe that will help business leaders to succeed, and at the same time to help resolve these seemingly intractable issues?'

We adopted a zero-base approach. We threw out all the conventional tasks of a leader and all those bits and pieces of duties, responsibilities, rituals and habits that adhere to them, like dust to a vacuum cleaner filter, and started with a clean sheet. We came to the conclusion that there were three basic areas which, when they become the leader's primary focus, can make an enormously liberating difference to his or her experience of the workplace.

Anticipate

Our work often feels like fire-fighting; struggling to come to terms with a constantly changing environment, running to catch up with the rapid advance of technology and hastily recalibrating our aims with customers and competitors who refuse to stay still for a moment. This sense of being behind the curve adds to feelings of stress and anxiety, and constantly generates challenges to our views of the world that can be unsettling and perhaps threatening. And worst of all, even when we realize we are behind the curve, most of us know that our attempts to do something will be hampered by organizational inertia and the time it takes to change investment priorities.

The solution is to get ahead of the curve, permanently. Part I of this book offered you tools and approaches that will help you to develop your own and your organization's ability to anticipate events. By adopting the approach and using the techniques of what we call 'skin-driven management', you will increase your alertness to 'weak signals', both from within and beyond the marketplace, and so create space to think ahead of the curve. Nurturing your mental agility with the tools provided in Chapter 2 will help you make best use of the space ahead of the curve your alertness creates, and should make sudden, unexpected changes in the business environment less threatening and easier to handle. And if you then take deliberate steps to loosen the bonds tying your resources to their current assignments, you can make things happen quicker (and it will feel less like walking through mud) when you have to respond to a weak signal you decide is important.

Align

The organization can be a lonely place if we are working long hours on something that doesn't really inspire us, and whose value to the world has not been clearly elucidated. Thrown together with people rushing about trying to make a living, and hoping to get home to the family at a reasonable hour, getting the job done can seem more important than your relationships at work. At an organizational level, undigested shareholder imperatives and mandates from head office can create an organization that is reactive and disempowered, rather than a high-performing environment that knows where it is going and cultivates strong *esprit de corps*.

In Part II we discussed our sense of being part of something beyond work: of our 'calling' or mission in life. We reflected on how to connect our personal goals with our business goals, and how such connection and congruence inspire trust and confidence among our colleagues and add to our personal charisma as leaders.

This feeling of alignment between what matters to you, and where you invest your time, shines out from you and strengthens you as a leader, and is also a necessary ingredient of a happy working life. Successful leaders embody their goals, and align all their beliefs, values, competencies and behaviours behind their calling as human beings, rather than merely as business leaders.

We discussed how personal relationships provide the synergy in organizations: the team can be more than the sum of its members. Alpha leaders know that they get results through people, and that people matter most.

We showed how alignment is needed at team and organizational levels, and we described how you can use alignment to assemble powerful coalitions and alliances that will deliver your business goals. We have all been involved with projects that get 'stuck', and initiatives that get bogged down in organizational resistance and inertia. Part II provided simple tools and approaches that will help you side-step these difficulties and deliver results.

Act

This is the part that helps you get your life back. Busy lives get full, and it is often hard to see the wood for the trees, to keep your priorities in view, to focus on where you, and only you, can make a difference. There is no rocket science in Part III, no stellar innovations, just quiet reminders of how to get the basics right, how to prioritize and take control of your life, how to be proactive in achieving your goals and how important it is to stick to those goals.

We propose a tactic of 'in-course correction' – to act, then adapt, rather than to wait for the perfect circumstances before moving forward. To keep ahead of the game, take action and improve as you go.

Focus on what is really important, and persist relentlessly until you have achieved your objectives – whether they are revenue targets, a brand position, new business process, or new behaviours 'in the muscle' of employees. This isn't sheer pig-headedness – you are applying the 'fixed purpose, responsive goals and flexible means' philosophy described in Chapter 2. To enable you to persist in your endeavours, eliminate all the initiatives that don't deliver high value. Less is more: do a little very well indeed.

Business leaders are widely regarded as having to sacrifice everything else for the job, and leaders who take normal holidays and work reasonable hours are often regarded as lacking 'the right stuff'. A relaxed business leader is almost a contradiction in terms. Unstinting diligence is one of the badges of modern business leaders, because it is evidence of commitment, and all the literature tells us that you can't have a committed workforce without a committed leader.

But there's no merit in diligence for its own sake. You can work extremely hard on tasks other people could do just as well as, if not better than, you and still be adding very little 'leadership value' to your organization. Alpha leaders do not spend a lot of time doing a lot of things; they spend a reasonable amount of time working in efficient ways on the things that really matter.

By working smart rather than hard you can retrieve the time you need to do what matters outside work, and you can recapture a balanced working life, where effectiveness is prioritized over diligence.

Of cults and cultures

There is a paradox at the heart of the idea of business leadership, which is that the leader must add value to the organization, but must not take it away when he or she leaves. An essential part of a leader's job is to make himself or herself dispensable through creating a *culture of leadership*, which extends throughout the organization.

When an organization becomes incapable and falls apart after the leader departs, the subsequent ruin is, in a sense, a corroboration of that leader's talent and evidence of the value added during his or her tenure. But it is also evidence of that leader's failure to endow the organization with the qualities needed to transcend previous achievements, the failure to nurture the conditions under which Alpha Leadership can flourish.

The most impressive organizations are those with a string of conspicuously able leaders. Tesco, one of the world's most admired grocery retailing groups, achieved leadership of the UK market under the stewardship of Ian McLaurin (now Lord McLaurin). When he retired, some predicted that Tesco's star would go into the descendent, but instead, under the leadership of Terry Leahy, it has gone from strength to strength. It is one of the few consumer goods retailing groups to have made a success of its international expansions in eastern Europe and the Far East, and at the time of writing it was the only consumer goods retailer in the world to have made money from Internet shopping. Safeway of the United States acknowledged this when it licensed Tesco's Internet shopping system.

Leahy is quite a different leader from McLaurin, but he would not have been so successful and become so admired in his own right if McLaurin had failed to ensure the legacy he left behind him was 'in the muscle' of the company.

Many of the qualities we have described in this book (sophisticated sensing systems to detect weak signals; 'skin-driven' management, cultures that can act, catalytic mechanisms) have the potential to be embedded in the muscle of the organization. But they will not become durable qualities that remain embedded in the muscle after the leader who introduced them leaves, if they are too intimately associated with that leader. It is one thing to get into the habit of behaving in ways you know your 'boss' wants you to behave, and quite another to behave in ways you know are right, irrespective of who the current leader is.

Other qualities we have described, such as mental agility, 'leading through embodiment', relationship management and dogged pursuit, are more personal, but they, too, if the philosophy behind them is sold effectively, can become attributes that a departing leader's successor steps into without thinking.

The distinction we are discussing here is between cult and culture. A cult is a rudimentary, incomplete, inherently ephemeral culture, that fades away when the personality that creates it departs. A culture is much more durable and robust than a cult, because its survival and power do not depend on the presence and personality of a single individual. It is shared, rather than imposed, by rhetoric and charisma, and can remain influential long after its creator has been forgotten. Some cults, such as Christianity, evolve into true cultures or religions. Some cults are clearly dysfunctional, and need to be dismantled and replaced when circumstances change.

The point is that if a leader's success is based on the power of his or her personality, his or her job is only half done. As the American journalist Walter Lippmann said: 'The final test of a leader is that he leaves behind him, in other men [and women], the conviction and the will to carry on.'[1] Alpha leaders develop other leaders as their successors – and develop wide-ranging *leadership* within their organizations.

The need to leave behind you a legacy of conviction and will obliges you to use the power of your personality with great care. Your objective should be to persuade people to follow you, not only because they admire and respect you, but also because they trust you to keep faith with the culture you and they share. You can contribute to, shape and cultivate the culture, but you will leave no durable legacy behind you if the organization does not learn to lead.

It is very tempting to rely largely on the power of your personality to get things done, because it is often the quickest way, and these days speed is crucial, particularly for company leaders whose average tenure is estimated to be between six and seven years. Why should you spend time and effort embedding attitudes, systems and behaviour patterns into the muscle of the organization, that you could spend on making acquisitions and restructuring its business portfolio? You have a limited amount of time to make a difference, after all, and capital markets are not well equipped to judge the value of durable and effective cultures, or pay due respect to the leaders who inspire their development.

But ask yourself what the people you leave behind will say of you after you are gone. Will the organization you led still be there to remember you, and if so, what position will you hold in the organization's memory? Will you be honoured like William L. McKnight at 3M, as the creator of a culture that still survives and was the platform for the company's sustained success, or will they just say that you 'held the fort' and did not do much damage?

Alpha Leaders have epitaphs and legacies in their minds, because their goal is not to win a few rounds in the endless game of business, while they hold the leader's baton, but to equip their organizations to go from strength to strength long after the baton has been passed on. What has the organization learned from you that will stand it in good stead in the future? Will you be able to say, when it seizes an opportunity its rivals failed to spot, or adapts more quickly than others to a new threat, 'I contributed to that'?

Circumstances and personalities differ, of course, and we recognize that no reader will feel all of the tools, techniques and approaches described and prescribed here are suitable and to their liking. There is no magic answer; no 'one size fits all' formula for transforming leaders' lives. But there's something here for everyone. We believe that even if you only apply some of the tools offered here, you will be a few steps further along the road to having greater impact as a leader, and to having a more enjoyable life.

Reference

Lippman, W. (1945) *New York Herald Tribune*.

www.AlphaLeaders.com

We have created the AlphaLeaders.com Website so that we can continue the conversation we began with you in this book about how to enhance your leadership presence and skills.

The **AlphaLeadership** project is an on-going conversation among us authors, and we are exploring ways to take this project forward. If you are interested in sharing your thoughts and views with us, we welcome your comments at AlphaLeaders.com.

Our Website includes:

- A discussion forum on Alpha Leadership issues
- A resource base for you as a leader
- Links to other leadership sites
- Easy-to-print resources designed for use in informal workshops with colleagues
- An opportunity to help us with our *next* book on Leadership and Life Balance
  - Do you know people who are really good examples of both leadership success and life balance?
  - Do you have an inspirational story or a horror story about work–life balance?
  - Does your firm have policies or approaches that greatly support high performance *and* life balance, or does it have a culture that encourages high performance at the expense of life balance?

We look forward to hearing from you.

Author biographies

Anne Deering
Vice President, A.T. Kearney Ltd

Anne Deering has 17 years experience as a management consultant with A.T. Kearney, working with senior executives to resolve complex business problems. A.T. Kearney is a global management consultancy, with 4000 employees worldwide.

She is responsible for the creation of Kearney's leadership development intellectual capital, working with both consulting and executive search teams.

She is asked to speak at conferences on leadership globally, for example July 2000 Tokyo ICM conference and May 2000 European Leadership Conference (Master Class for 150 leading CEOs from around Europe). Sky Business News, CNN, CNBC, *The Financial Times*, *Time*, and *Le Figaro* have interviewed her on leadership topics.

Her consulting experience in Europe and North America has been primarily in the areas of leadership and team development, organizational learning, organization redesign and strategy.

She is co-author of *The Difference Engine*, a research-based book on partnering approaches and techniques (published by Gower, 1998). *The Difference Engine* was short-listed for the business management book of the year award in 1999 by the Institute of Management Consultants.

She holds a BSc in Psychology and a BA (Oxon) in English Language and Literature. She has a Diploma of Management Studies and European Marketing. She also holds the Diploma of the Chartered Institute of Marketing and the Diploma of the Institute of Linguists (Spanish).

Anne Deering
A.T. Kearney Ltd
Lansdowne House
Berkeley Square
London W1X 5DH
Tel: 44 (0)207 468 8029
Fax: 44 (0)207 468 8103
anne.deering@atkearney.com
http://www.atkearney.com

Robert Dilts
Co-founder of Dilts Strategy Group and ISVOR Dilts

Robert Dilts has had a global reputation as a leading behavioural skills trainer and business consultant since the late 1970s. He consults and trains on leadership and organizational development throughout the world to a wide variety of professional groups and organizations. Past clients and sponsors have included Apple Computers, Hewlett-Packard, IBM, The World Bank, Alitalia, Telecom Italia, Lucasfilms Ltd, Ernst & Young, The American Society for Training and Development and the State Railway of Italy. He has lectured extensively on leadership, organizational learning and change management, making presentations and keynote addresses for The European Forum for Quality Management, The World Health Organization and Harvard University. Robert has worked with Fiat since 1988, helping to develop programmes on leadership, innovation, values and systemic thinking. He is currently an associate professor at the Fiat School of Management and has been extensively involved in the development of the new Fiat Leadership Model.

Robert has been a developer, author, trainer and consultant in the field of neuro-linguistic programming (NLP) – a model of human behaviour, learning and communication – since its creation in 1975 by John Grinder and Richard Bandler. A long-time student and colleague of both Grinder and Bandler, Robert also studied personally with Milton H. Erickson, MD, and Gregory Bateson. In addition to spearheading the applications of NLP to education, creativity, health and leadership, his personal contributions to the field of NLP include much of the ground-breaking work on the NLP techniques of Strategies and Belief Systems, and the development of what has become known as 'Systemic NLP'.

Robert has a degree in Behavioural Technology from the University of California at Santa Cruz. He received the President's Undergraduate Fellowship in 1977 for research correlating eye movement and brain function conducted at the Langley Porter Neuropsychiatric Institute in San Francisco.

Robert is the principal author of *Neuro-Linguistic Programming Vol. I* (with John Grinder, Richard Bandler and Judith DeLozier, 1980), which serves as the standard reference text for the field. He has authored numerous other books, including: *Skills for the Future* (with Gino Bonissone, 1993); *Strategies of Genius Vols. I–III* (1994–95); *Visionary Leadership Skills* (1996); *Modeling with NLP* (1998); *Sleight of Mouth* (1999), describing the set of verbal reframing patterns he developed to influence beliefs conversationally. His most recent book (co-authored with Judith DeLozier) is the *Encyclopedia of Systemic Neuro-Linguistic Programming and NLP New Coding*, published in 2000.

Robert Dilts
ISVOR DILTS Leadership Systems, Inc.
One Bay Plaza
1350 Old Bayshore Highway, Suite 700
Burlingame, CA 94010
Tel: 1 650-558-4140
Fax: 1 650-558-4147
rdilts@nlpu.com
http://www.isvordilts.com

Julian Russell
Managing Director, PPD Consulting Ltd

Julian Russell has over 20 years experience as a personal development expert and leadership coach. He has been described as the 'executive coach who gets to the parts other personal development can't reach'. He is dedicated to helping leaders and teams operate at their very best, increasing value in the organization while also enhancing their own sense of wellbeing and personal satisfaction.

He specializes in helping leaders develop a sense of personal alignment which generates charisma or presence, stimulating people to follow with enthusiasm. When this personal power is combined with a real understanding of what motivates and influences people, then great things can happen.

Julian has been the Managing Director of PPD Consulting Ltd, a coaching and development firm for senior executives, since 1995. He presents regularly at conferences and coaches a select number of leaders to help them develop their leadership style.

Clients include Airtours, American Express, Bank of New York, Barclays Bank, Cranfield University, Deutsche Bank, Discovery Channel, EDS, Financial Times, Morgan Stanley, National Grid, PricewaterhouseCoopers, Prudential, Rolls-Royce Motor Cars, Royal Bank of Scotland, Shell, Thames Water and Whitbread, among others.

His business life started as assistant to the Managing Director of Moet & Chandon (London) Ltd in 1978, after which he switched careers and became the director of a personal development organization, Nucleus Network. From 1983 he worked as consultant on a variety of personal developments and human communication projects, including helping to fund voluntary sector personal development organizations for the Artemis Trust; the first business-consulting project in Britain using neuro-linguistic programming in 1985; and the pilot studies for a business training company using NLP.

Julian founded Pace Personal Development Ltd in 1988, one of the premier NLP training organizations in the UK, and was for many years the only trainer in the UK to have been personally trained by one of the founders of NLP. He joined the Board of the Association for NLP and became a trustee of Revision, a psychotherapy training charity. He was the first NLP trainer to teach in the former Soviet Union at the invitation of the Soviet Academy of Science. He is a UKCP registered psychotherapist.

Julian has written a handbook on *Spreading Personal Growth in Society* (Artemis Trust, UK, 1985), and has contributed a chapter on leadership to a forthcoming book on self relations psychology edited by Steve Gilligan, to be published in 2003.

Julian Russell
Managing Director
PPD Consulting Ltd
Arundel House
31a St James's Square
London SW1Y 4JR
Tel: 44 (0)207 665 1677
Fax: 44 (0)207 665 1777
Julian.Russell@ppdconsulting.com
http://www.ppdconsulting.com

Listing of references for Part and Chapter opening epigraphs

Part 1: Kelly, Kevin, *New Rules for the New Economy: 10 Ways the Network Economy is Changing Everything*, Fourth Estate, 1999.

Chapter 1: Kelly, Kevin, *New Rules for the New Economy: 10 Ways the Network Economy is Changing Everything*, Fourth Estate, 1999.

Chapter 2: Einstein, Albert, on Science.

Chapter 3: Foster, Alan Dean, *To the Vanishing Point*, Wildside Press, 1999.

Part II: Wheatley, Margaret J., *Leadership and the New Science: Discovering Order in a Chaotic World*, Berrett-Koehler Publishers, 2001.

Chapter 4: Shakespeare, William, *Hamlet, Prince of Denmark*, c. 1601 (Act I, Scene iii, line 82), Cambridge University Press, 1985.

Chapter 5: Forster, E. M., *Howard's End*, 1910 (Chapter 22), Penguin Books, 2000.

Chapter 6: Montague, Charles Edward, *Disenchantment*, Greenwood Press, 1978.

Part III: A proverb from Papua New Guinea.

Chapter 7: A principle commended in the biblical book of *Proverbs* (e.g. 24:27). Also the title of a book by G. Jackson, subtitled *Addresses to Young Men*, 1894.

Chapter 8: Emerson, Ralph Waldo, *Prudence*, included in *Essays by Ralph Waldo Emerson: First Series*, HarperCollins, 1981.

Chapter 9: Fields, W. C., quoted in *Halliwell's Film Quiz Book*, edited by Andrew Murray and John Walker, HarperCollins Entertainment, 2000.

Chapter 10: Pompadour, Madam De, quoted in *Mémoires de Madame du Hausset*, 1824, p. 19.

Index